THE AUSTRALIAN

Women's Weekly

the cook's garden

acp
books

CONTENTS

planning for production

A cook's garden supplies the special plants that cooks love to use. To have on hand those special textures and tastes, fresh and lush from the garden, grown as you like them, harvested at the peak of perfection and in just the quantity you need – that's what an ideal cook's garden provides.

A gardener's garden contains fine and carefully cultivated specimens of seasonal fruit and vegetables, planted in neat, regular rows – as dictated by time-honoured books, and usually cooked by equally time-honoured methods – they're rewarding, productive and an economic boon to the family. And there's nothing wrong with that.

But the cook's garden has more subtle supplies: a bit of this, a trial of that, a few seasonal stars, a little something happy in a pot or among the flowers. The cook's garden helps you add a bit of magic to a meal. It's that happy mix that lets you turn cooking into creation.

Your cook's garden will no doubt include many collected treasures from other cooks' gardens: some saved seeds, a piece broken off to strike, or a snippet of something shared after a successful trial. Most likely there'll be seed trays, cuttings of 'new' varieties in pots ready to plant into the garden proper, an assembly of herbs at the ready, and various experiments with unusual shapes and colours. There's always the chance that some of these new varieties will become kitchen standards, and you'll wonder how you ever lived without them.

But, of course, dreams are dreams. The dictates of climate and available space are the controllers of what becomes reality in your garden. Being able to get your hands on just the right plants can sometimes be a bit of a struggle. You'll see glorious pictures in gardening books and strange varieties in shops, and wonder where you can get seedlings to grow your own. And then there's time, alas, so often in very short supply.

The Cook's Garden is for those ready to bridge the divide between the great kitchen indoors and the great garden outdoors, and wanting to create their own unique kitchen garden.

Let's look at suggestions to help you down the garden path with your arms loaded or your fist proudly wrapped round something garden-fresh for your table.

dictates of climate

Choosing the wrong plants for your climate will make gardening more difficult than it actually is.

Of course, we all want to grow a lemon or a lime, quinces or nuts, asparagus or raspberries, melons or things that tempt us but, in reality, some are climatically impossible. Some of us will take up the challenge; attempt to create the right microclimate with wind, shade or sun barriers, even moving large pots about. Sometimes we succeed, but more often it's a huge struggle for, most likely, a meagre result.

It is much wiser to accept the limitations of your particular garden conditions and choose those fruit and vegetables that grow well. You'll find that, in any climate range, you'll still have a considerable choice of fruits, herbs, flowers and vegetables.

dictates of space

Some lucky gardeners have large vegetable plots with space for everything. Make no mistake, though, such gardens are a lot of work, both in preparation and maintenance. Other gardeners take advantage of tiny spaces, such as a patch of concrete, a balcony or a collection of pots, and still manage to grow herbs and vegetables – things that a cook needs to add a special flavour, a decorative flourish and a home-grown touch.

A cook's garden can be as large or as small as you have space, time and the inclination for working in it. Also, when time is short, a small garden can be infinitely more rewarding and successful than a large, ambitious garden that takes up so much time and energy that it most often ends up abandoned.

year-round harvest

Undoubtedly, one of the genuine joys of home gardening is the thrill of enjoying vegetables and fruit in season and at their best. Supermarket shopping has dulled and denied our appreciation of such gastronomic thrills as new-season pears and peaches, fresh baby potatoes, vine-ripened tomatoes and fresh strawberries.

A carefully designed cook's garden, however small, can yield favourite fruits and vegetables for a varied and colourful seasonal table. The enthusiastic cook with a kitchen garden at the ready will rise to the cooking challenge and explore the wonderful world of fresh herbs and home-grown produce.

The possibilities of small spaces

Forget the segregation of vegetables into beds. Herbs, vegetables and flowers can all be grown together for stunning visual displays.

Get rid of the lawn Dig it up, removing all the roots or they'll reach up through your garden and steal valuable water and nutrients. A sea of herbs and vegetables looks twice as good as a featureless area of grass.

Take advantage of height Grow climbers like peas, cucumbers and beans on tripods among floral displays. Nasturtiums can clamber among them too. Let unstaked mini tomatoes wander among tall shrubs.

Mix colours Bright chillies look stunning among flowers, and the red and yellow stems of ruby silver beet (chard) are equally striking. Grey-leafed vegetables like artichokes, broccoli and sage extend the colour palette, so do purple-leafed beauties like beetroot, basil and beans.

plant supplies

The easiest way to acquire seeds and plants is, of course, to buy them from local nurseries. This way, you'll always buy what's in season for your area. Choose the healthiest looking plants; green, not lanky or leaning, still growing robustly and not in flower.

It's also easy and inexpensive to raise seeds from packets. Use a special seed-raising compost, and in cold, frosty climates, start seedlings early indoors or under glass. Or save your own seeds from the last year's harvest (provided, of course, they are not hybrid forms) and the seeds will germinate next year.

potted plants

Choose pots that are big enough to easily hold the mass of roots that are to fill them, or they'll be forever thirsty and weak. They need to be 10cm (4") wider and deeper than the root ball.

Terracotta is impressive but expensive. Plastic pots are cheap, and they don't dry out as quickly, but will blow over and deteriorate with exposure to the sun. Metal or wooden containers, like buckets, a wheel-barrow or half-barrel, will do a perfect job as a pot, but must have holes for drainage. Wooden crates and polystyrene boxes have also been successfully used as pots.

Most trees will grow in pots but not to full size because their roots are restricted. Citrus trees are often potted. Olives are very content to grow in pots, so too are figs and bay trees. Miniature varieties of apples, peaches, nectarines and

cherries are also ideal, although they all need careful maintenance. Herbs are excellent potted plants as most of them love good drainage. Choose pots that suit their shape: tall herbs like dill, rosemary or tarragon look good in tall, wide pots; weeping types like thyme or savoury are better suited to cascading on their own over pots 15-20cm (6-8") high, or as borders to the mound-shaped sage, basil, parsley or marjoram. Mint, both standard and Vietnamese varieties, is best confined to a pot because it's so invasive. Chervil can be moved into semi-shade during the hottest part of the year.

Tomatoes, especially mini varieties, make excellent pot specimens, but demand large pots to accommodate their roots. Peppers, cucumbers, chillies, all the leafy green crops and beans do well in pots, as will winter vegetables like broccoli or mini cauliflower and peas.

Mix leaf shapes and forms The solid and textural greenness of silver beet, curly-leafed kale or carrots offers a good contrast to floral colour. Lemon grass provides a wonderful grassy profile.

Use vegetables and herbs as borders Chives, mignonette lettuce, oregano and radish make good edging plants, and team happily with violas, dwarf nasturtiums and alyssum.

Don't forget vertical surfaces Cover fences with wire, twine or lattice for beans, peas, marrows, cucumber, melons or grapes.

Don't let concrete deter you Tiny pockets of soil can be created by building up garden beds using rocks, wood or bricks to create well-drained spots beside steps or even straight onto concrete. Such raised beds will happily accommodate herbs and salad greens.

cultivation for success

soil types

There's no denying the major requirement for success with producing crops is the condition of the soil. There are two major soil types: clay and sand, and your soil will be at one or the other of these two ends of the scale, or it may be somewhere in between, where the quantities of sand, clay and organic material are mixed.

Clay is fine-particled, hard when dry and sticky when wet. Clay soils have good supplies of the minerals and essential elements necessary for plant growth, but little space for air, water and the roots to move through. To break up these heavy soils, spread on gypsum (available from your local nursery or agricultural supply store), leave for a month, then dig in large quantities of organic matter, like compost and manure.

A short-cut technique is to spread gypsum, add a layer of pelleted poultry manure, and then build a garden bed on top of this, raised enough to allow room for root growth. Use garden soil mix, well-aged manure and compost mixed together. This is all you need to grow the first crop. The following season it can be dug in and combined with the underlying clay. Add more organic matter each season. Soil that is just moist is easiest and best to dig.

Sand has large particles visible to the naked eye. The soil will not compact, even when squeezed. Air (essential for the roots), fills the gaps, but water (essential for the whole plant) drains away too rapidly. To slow down the rate of water loss, and to increase the nutrient- and mineral-holding capacity, add large quantities of manure and well-rotted compost.

The middle group, the **loams**, are sand or clay mixed with enough organic material to make them workable – they are the ideal garden soil. But even they need regular applications of manure and compost if they are to remain productive.

fertilisers

Vegetables fall into three groups: leafy types, flowering/fruiting varieties and root crops. They all have their own preferences for essential elements.

Leafy vegetables and herbs (for example, spinach, lettuce, basil, cabbage) need large amounts of nitrogen (N) for vigorous growth and abundant foliage.

Flowering/fruiting varieties are those that grow a container of seeds (for example, pumpkin, peas, cucumbers and tomatoes). Their special requirement is potassium (K) to boost flowering.

Root vegetables require good supplies of phosphorus (P) for vigorous root development.

There are two choices of fertiliser: chemical or organic.

Chemical fertilisers are constructed artificially by combining elements to correct specific problems such as magnesium, phosphorus or potassium deficiencies, or mixed to suit specific plant varieties. There are also complete plant foods, with a mix of all the elements for healthy plant growth. These are the most suitable for vegetable growth. They are mixed into the soil before planting time to avoid chemical burning of seedling roots.

Soluble fertilisers are dissolved in water and, when applied, are taken up immediately by both the leaves and roots. Slow-release pelleted formulas are a more gentle method of providing nutrients, and less likely to shock plants.

For all of them, use only the quantities recommended on the package as overload will kill the plants. The only additional need is nitrogen boosts in liquid dressings for leafy vegetables.

Organic fertilisers provide required elements in natural form and will not build up deposits of unused chemical salts in the soil. They are available as slow-release pelleted poultry manure (with a nutrient composition similar to the complete plant foods), or blood, fish and bone meal. All organic fertilisers are slow-release formulas as they must decompose before the nutrients are available.

Seaweed and fish emulsions are foliar organic sprays and there are also other manure- or plant-derived mixes that can be blended at home. Their nutrients are available immediately.

Manures are not fertilisers but soil improvers. They help provide the light, airy composition required, but their nutrient benefits are low. Manures must be well decomposed before seedlings are put in as the process of breaking down can kill the plants. Spread it on the garden a month before planting or spread it out in sunlight until it loses its strong aroma. It's then safe to use.

There are other soil conditions, like acidity or alkalinity (the pH), that influence how plants grow. In most gardens the soil pH is not a problem, but by varying the sources of organic matter used, you'll prevent any imbalances developing. Should problems arise, buy an inexpensive soil testing kit from a garden centre, take several samples in your garden and send it to the laboratory to be tested.

Worm farms

Worm farms are a form of kitchen and garden waste recycling. They put to good use the incredible ability of earthworms to digest and decompose organic matter. You will need a three-layered stack of plastic trays (available as a kit from hardware shops and garden suppliers) and a large supply of worms. It's an odour-free and efficient way to recycle kitchen waste. The upper layer houses the worms in moist peat beds and here you add kitchen refuse, vegetable peelings, leftovers, leaf debris from the garden, coffee grains, tea leaves, shredded paper, etc. (Worms don't like onion or citrus skins or meat waste.) The second layer collects the worm castings, or vermicast, the nutrient-rich by-product of their digestive processes. This can be spread over the garden as mulch or used to raise seedlings. The bottom layer collects an equally valuable liquid that can be used as a liquid fertiliser, neat for established plants or diluted to half strength for seedlings. It's recycling at its best.

potting plants

planting out pots

Good soil and constant watering are essential, no matter what pot you use. Normal garden soil can't be used. Well-matured compost is alright, but reduces in volume over time and requires topping up. Commercial potting mixes are the other alternative. Buy the best you can afford.

Gravel or pottery shards in the base of a pot improve drainage. Put in a 10-15cm (4-6") layer of potting compost over the base, place the root ball on top, fill around the sides and add a light layer of compost. The plant should sit 2.5cm (1") below the rim. Add slow-release fertiliser at the recommended rate and later, make regular light sprays with a foliar feed to keep plants robust.

re-potting

For small pots, replace the mix for each new planting. For large pots, dig the soil well and add fertiliser and top-ups of compost to keep the mix light.

Re-pot plants when they become root-bound. If small enough to handle, pull the dampened plant from the pot and carve away some of the roots. Replace in new compost and prune to keep the top and bottom in proportion. Water well and start the fertiliser regime two weeks later.

watering pots

It's so easy to forget to water your plants. Potted plants dry out very quickly, and one day you'll come home to dead treasures on the doorstep. If you're busy, a watering system is a great boon, and friendly neighbours are essential when you go away.

Don't stand pots permanently in water-filled saucers as their roots rot. It can be an emergency measure for weekends away, but make sure you take them out as soon as you return.

The no-dig garden

This is a very productive form of gardening, but it does require heavy work to set up. It can be used for problems like weed-ridden, rocky or severely compacted soils, and even over concrete. Wood, bricks, garden walling and sleepers can be used to frame a garden bed. The bed must be strong enough to bear the weight of wet fillings and 1.2m (4') high to accommodate roots.

soil-based sites

Build up the following layers:

1 Light cover of pelleted poultry manure

2 5cm (2") layer of damp newspaper

3 Complete layer of spent mushroom compost

4 10cm (4") layer of chicken manure

5 20cm (8") thick layer of straw

6 Another layer of pelleted poultry manure

7 10cm (4") layer of straw.

Water well and plant into pockets of compost placed into hollows made in the top layer of straw.

concrete or paved sites

Start with a 5cm (2") layer of dried straw then add layers 4-6 above. Add another layer of dried straw topped with layers 4-6. Repeat the layers until the garden is 2-3cm (2") below the top of the bed. Do not dig and disturb the layers. Place plants into compost pockets in the top layer of straw and keep the bed well watered. After each harvest, add compost to top-up, but eventually replace the whole structure when the level falls low enough to fit in layers 3-7.

pests and pest control

insects

After slugs and snails, insects are the most significant pests, including aphids and whitefly which can be controlled with proprietary systemic pesticides. Always follow the instructions on the label.

Insect-proof mesh and fleece help to prevent an infestation of caterpillars and butterflies, and will help to advance the crop.

diseases

Wet warm weather encourages downy mildews so good plant spacing, and burning of affected foliage is vital to limit its spread. In fact, providing plants with good growing conditions helps them to resist physiological disorders and fend off pests and diseases. Potato blight is treated with copper fungicides allowing a two-week delay in the destruction of potato foliage.

biological control

Using living creatures to control pests is widely practised in greenhouses and insect parasitic nematodes are offered for a wide range of pests.

It is costly for manufacturers to develop and get approval for pesticides so few are offered to gardeners, and few are mentioned here – the information and proprietary names would become out of date quickly.

crop rotation

Rotating crops ensures that the nutrients added to the soil by one plant are available to subsequent plants. For example, legumes trap nitrogen in nodules on their roots. Leafy vegetables, which need large quantities of nitrogen, will benefit from the added nitrogen if planted after legumes.

Likewise, root vegetables planted after leafy vegetables will utilise the phosphorus not needed by the leafy vegetables. Fruiting plants such as tomatoes, peas, cucumbers, and the like, will make use of spare potassium.

Crop rotating ensures soil-living pests and diseases favouring one plant group cannot build up in the one spot. Gardening in this manner, though requiring planning and knowledge, means that all the nutrients in the soil are used and the garden is worked to maximum effect.

companion planting

Some plants grow better if you plant them alongside each other. United, they support, shelter and provide root space and nutrients for each other. Some herbs deter insect pests.

A careful selection of plants and companions means that you can grow much variety within a small space while at the same time you help control pests. Nor are insect infestations likely to reach plague proportions as they can easily do in larger, single-crop garden beds.

Here are some well-known plant combinations:

Beans grow more strongly with summer savoury and when planted alternately with corn; however, they are not too fond of garlic or onions.

Cabbage, cauliflower and **broccoli** get protection from cabbage moth when planted near celery, sage or rosemary.

Peas and **broad beans** are protected from aphids by calendula, which attract hover flies that eat aphids.

Nasturtiums repel aphids among **peas**, and beetles among **pumpkins** and **cucumbers**.

Potatoes are more disease-resistant when planted among horseradish and, when planted with beans, are less likely to suffer beetle damage.

Tomatoes have more flavour when grown near basil and develop more vigorously when planted near marigolds.

Plant **carrots** and **onions** together and the pungent smell of the onions will help keep pests out of the fine feathery leaves of carrots.

Sage helps repel cabbage butterfly; **thyme** helps repel cabbage root fly. **Dill** attracts a wasp to control cabbage moth when planted near brassicas. **Rosemary** deters cabbage moth and carrot fly.

compost

Compost is a very effective system for recycling and reducing garden waste; it reproduces in the garden what happens in nature where vegetable matter decomposes and returns to the soil. There is no mystery about composting. You can, if you want, simply pile waste on open ground and wait.

However, the whole process is sped up if you build a wooden- or wire-sided container 1m (3') high. Make sure your compost pile is in the sun, there is earth beneath, air and water can penetrate and there is easy access. Add kitchen waste, non-diseased garden waste, shredded paper, even hair and vacuum cleaner contents. The rule is that, if it was once alive, it is suitable to compost.

Avoid bones and meat waste as they encourage scavengers and flies. Between each addition, add layers of lawn clippings or leaves. Herbs (comfrey, yarrow and tansy) and blood and bone will speed up the composting process. When full, the pile can be turned and left to mature. You can then begin a new compost pile and the original will be usable in 3-4 months.

For city gardens, plastic bins with lids are recommended as they take up less space, don't attract vermin and don't look unsightly.

pests and diseases

The first step in managing garden pests is to accurately diagnose them. Infestations of leaf-eating insects are easy to identify. Caterpillars can be found on or under leaves making inroads into them. Some beetles chew leaves as well.

Chemical sprays will kill insects and unwanted pests, but can be harmful to humans and beneficial to insects. It's wiser to kill them by hand (which is possible in a kitchen garden) or treat with crop-safe sprays bought specifically for the problem from a garden centre.

Chemical baits are available for slugs and snails, as are safe, organic alternatives such as beer traps and grapefruit halves. Alternatively, gather them by hand at night and tread on them or drown them in a mix of water and detergent, kill them as they drink from saucers of alcohol or milk, or make barriers using grit, copper or sawdust.

Sap-sucking insects range from minute dots (thrips), to moving masses (aphids), static hard pinheads (scales), small flies (white fly) to beetles.

There are commercial chemical treatments for all of these pests, but if you wish to remain organic, crush by hand where possible, or blast off with water.

Other leaf problems include rust, fungus and mildew. These will cover then, eventually, kill the leaves. Commercial sprays will save the plant and stop the spread of spores if used early enough. Destroy the infected foliage and stems rather than adding to the compost heap, in order to prevent spreading the problem elsewhere.

Soil fungus can be reduced in small areas by pouring on boiling water prior to planting. Check first that the soil is not full of active worms.

Collect stem-eating grubs in the soil during the day and at night when they are active on the surface. Marigolds repel grubs and nematodes for several metres.

Fruit-fly needs special attention. Chemical treatments should be used to stop their spread. Don't leave dropped fruit on the ground where the fruit-fly larvae pupate. Collect and boil, or seal in plastic bags and 'cook' any damaged fruit in the sun.

the spring garden

spring is the season of anticipation

Even though the calendar may announce its arrival, often the weather does not. We usually get the odd hot spring day, a foretaste of languid summer making us anticipate its delights, and then the next day there's a sharp, cold reminder to bring us back to reality. However, it's the lengthening daylight hours that summer-growing plants respond to, so don't despair if chilly winds blow.

If space is not a problem, leave garden beds fallow over winter, covered in manure and mulch. They will be ready for planting in spring. Areas shaded in winter are best revitalised in this way.

Most city gardens don't have the luxury of space. To make room for spring, clear existing beds, remove ragged, tired-looking plants that are no longer productive and, above all, be inventive with your plant combinations and space-saving ideas. Compost all debris; chop up tough stems to speed up decomposition.

Plants start to grow because they have to; they've been beckoned. The leaves and buds unfurl with splashes of subtle colour, and the full display of spring flowers strengthens as the season takes hold. In a corner of the vegetable garden, asparagus responds to the directive, bees are heard among the peas, and the broad beans flower. Tarragon and chives obey the command and wave their leaves in the breeze like banners.

Save wizened bean or pea pods and store for the next sowing. Dig up clods and break up roots in the soil. Add well-rotted compost.

Early-bird gardeners will have already raised tomato, basil, pepper and courgette seedlings under cover during late winter, or will have been down to the local nursery for seedlings. Gardeners in frost-prone areas must time their planting out carefully so that they can avoid tricky, late frosts.

Now, your most difficult gardening decision is whether to plant favourites or new varieties. All are worth a try. Remember, good soil preparation, combination planting and crop rotation will ensure an abundant and wonderfully diverse kitchen garden.

It's time to plant okra if you have a warm greenhouse.

sow now	harvest now
vegetables aubergines, beetroot, broad beans, broccoli, Brussels sprouts, cabbage, carrots, cauliflowers, courgettes, cucumber, endive, leeks, lettuce, onions, peas, radicchio, silver beet, spinach	**vegetables** asparagus, broad beans, spring cabbage, carrots, cauliflowers, garlic, kale, lettuce, radishes, rhubarb, rocket, spinach
herbs basil, chives, coriander, dill, fennel, marjoram, parsley, sage, thyme	**fruit** rhubarb, strawberries

garden peas

You might consider it useless growing peas when the frozen alternative is so convenient, but the flavour of a just-picked pea makes it all worthwhile. Like sweet corn, peas have a high-sugar content, which slowly converts to starch after picking. If you gather peas young and eat them straight from the plant, you can really taste the difference. Today's gardener can grow many kinds of peas. Snow peas (or mange tout) and sugar snap peas are now as well known as regular green peas. Also try unusual varieties like wrinkled peas – said to have superior flavour – and winged, or asparagus, peas for something completely different. In a small kitchen garden, you'll be able to grow enough for a small harvest once or twice a week; in a large garden you'll have supplies to freeze or give away.

in the garden

Peas take around 12-16 weeks to mature from sowing to harvesting in the UK, depending on your location. Choose a sunny site, and sow every four weeks from early spring to the start of summer. The plants are frost-tolerant but the flowers and young pods are not, so protect early crops from frosts. In warmer gardens, peas make a useful winter crop.

Prepare a well-drained and sunny site by digging over well. As weed removal is difficult between seedlings, a mulch mat on either side of the rows or in the centre and around the outside of a tripod should help. Leave a 2cm (1") gap for the seeds. Put down slow-release fertiliser or blood and bone and cover it with a 3cm (1¼") thick layer of damp newspaper, spreading 10cm (4") beyond the seed position. Gravel will hide it and stop it blowing away. The weeds can't break through until the paper disintegrates and the pea roots can reach the fertiliser right through their growth.

Put in stakes and wire or twine for row planting, and tripod supports and connecting twine if growing in teepee shapes.

Peas grow 2m (6') high. Wet the soil and plant the seeds 5cm (2") deep so birds and mice won't find them, spacing them about 10cm (4") apart if they are to grow up frames or poles, closer if they're self-supporting on the ground. Seedlings will break through in about a week, taking longer if the soil is cool.

Water the seedlings regularly after they emerge. The flowers will start in a couple of months and pods a week later. Don't let the pods grow too big as the peas will be mealy and the plants will stop producing. The more you pick, the more the plants produce.

Peas for shelling should have space between each pea and the pod shouldn't be tight. Peas eaten in the pod (snow peas and sugar snap peas) should be pliable, about 8cm (3") long with small pea formations.

At the end of the season, cut off the stems at ground level and compost undiseased stems and leaves. Leave the roots and their nitrogen nodules in the ground for a crop of lettuce or silver beet to use.

preserving the crop

STORING	All peas should be eaten as soon as possible after picking. If they must be stored, rinse and dry thoroughly on absorbent paper and store in the refrigerator. Don't pod peas until you are ready to cook them.
FREEZING	An oversupply of green peas can be blanched and frozen (see Freezing, page 113). Sugar snap peas and snow peas do not freeze well; but a pea puree will, so cook the peas, puree, then freeze.

pests and diseases

Problems include pea moth (which lays its egg to be discovered later in the pods); aphids; hose off, crush between your fingers or spray with pyrethrum sprays. Another problem is mildew, which can kill pea plants. Use a commercial spray that won't harm bees, peas or predators.

for the table

to prepare

• Sugar snap peas and snow peas need very little cooking. Add to boiling water and cook until they just change colour. If they are for salads, remove and cool in iced water.

• Green peas require slightly more cooking, and older peas require a longer time, generally about 2-4 minutes. Don't overcook as this toughens peas. Never add bicarbonate of soda to the water. The peas stay green, but you destroy their nutritional value.

to serve

• Fresh pea soup is fantastic. Cook peas in chicken stock and blend with the pulp from a roasted bulb of garlic. Stir in cream or more chicken stock if necessary. Add snipped chives, salt and pepper. Serve chilled or hot.

• Secure blanched snow peas around cooked prawns with toothpicks and serve with a chilli-soy dipping sauce.

• Serve green peas, sugar snap peas and snow peas tossed through a little gremolata (a mixture of garlic, lemon rind and parsley).

• Fry fine bacon strips until crisp, add a little balsamic vinegar and some blanched sugar snap peas.

• Both sugar snap peas and snow peas, when lightly blanched, can be used as crudités. They are particularly good served with bagna cauda (an Italian, warm garlic and anchovy dip/sauce served and consumed in a manner similar to fondue).

• For a spring salad, toss any blanched peas with lettuce, asparagus tips, spring onions, chervil and parsley leaves; dress with a vinaigrette and add crumbled blue cheese.

• Try tossing a pea pesto through spaghetti instead of basil pesto. Just microwave 2 cups frozen peas until tender; drain and process with 2 garlic cloves, a handful of pine nuts and mint leaves, about ½ cup each of basil leaves and Parmesan cheese. Slowly pour in 2 tablespoons olive oil and blend until mixture forms a thick puree. Toss through cooked spaghetti and add some crispy pancetta.

• For a delicious summer salad, tear the leaves of a butter lettuce, cos lettuce and red oak leaf lettuce and toss in a large bowl with 2 cups of snow pea sprouts, 3 sliced avocados and 3 sliced peaches. Dress with a simple balsamic vinaigrette.

green peas

sugar snap peas

mange tout or snow peas

snow pea sprouts

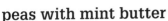

peas with mint butter

2¼ cups (350g) fresh shelled peas

40g butter, softened

1 tablespoon finely chopped fresh mint

1 teaspoon finely grated lemon rind

1 Boil, steam or microwave peas until tender; drain.

2 Meanwhile, combine remaining ingredients in small bowl.

3 Serve peas topped with butter mixture.

prep+ cook time 10 minutes **serves** 4

caramelised aubergine with snow peas

2 large aubergines (1kg), halved lengthways, sliced thickly

1⅓ cups (330ml) water

⅔ cup (130g) jasmine rice, rinsed, drained

200g snow peas, trimmed

2 tablespoons mirin

2 tablespoons Japanese soy sauce

2 teaspoons light brown sugar

2cm piece fresh ginger (10g), grated finely

1 tablespoon toasted sesame seeds

1 Cook aubergines in large baking-paper-lined steamer, over large saucepan of simmering water, about 15 minutes or until tender.

2 Bring the water to the boil, covered, in medium saucepan; Add rice; cook, covered, over low heat, 10 minutes. Remove from heat; stand, covered, 10 minutes. Fluff rice with fork.

3 Boil, steam or microwave peas until tender; drain.

4 Combine mirin, sauce, sugar and ginger in a large frying pan; bring to the boil. Add half the aubergines; cook over medium heat until aubergine caramelises. Transfer to heatproof bowl; cover to keep warm. Repeat with remaining aubergines.

5 Divide rice into serving bowls; top with snow peas and aubergines, sprinkle with sesame seeds.

prep + cook time 30 minutes **serves** 4

potatoes

Rare is the person who doesn't eat potatoes, whether as chips or mashed. Nor is a potato merely a potato these days. A shopping trip means negotiating such names as 'Pontiac', 'Desiree', 'Pink Fir Apple' and 'King Edward', all with their different textures, tastes and colours. Many gardeners grow potatoes as they are well worth the effort and easy to propagate. Keep a few of your favourite varieties, let them sprout, then grow your own. All you need is a sunny, well-drained site and enough room.

in the garden

Potatoes must be grown in frost-free conditions, so plant away from frost pockets. They can be planted all year where winter conditions are mild. For an early crop, warm the soil with plastic before planting in late winter under fleece.

Select a sunny, well-drained position. If the soil was not manured for the previous crop, add compost so the soil is light. Break up heavy clods. Don't add lime, but do add a complete or slow-release organic fertiliser.

Potatoes grow from whole potatoes or small pieces (golf-ball size) that have started to sprout. You can sprout your own (just keep until shoots form) or buy seed potatoes from nurseries (guaranteed virus-free, which is important if you've had dieback problems with potatoes or related crops such as tomatoes, peppers and aubergines).

Make a furrow about 15cm (6") deep and position the potato pieces about 40cm (16") apart, with their 'eyes' or sprouts facing up. Backfill with fine soil and mulch to reduce weeds and late-frost damage.

When the leafy stems are about 20cm (8") tall, earth up the soil to about 5cm (2") below the top of the stem on each plant, creating furrows between them. Earthing up encourages more stems to develop and hence more potatoes. It also prevents light reaching the potato tubers – when exposed to light they turn green and are poisonous.

Potatoes need regular watering to keep the tubers well-shaped and smooth-skinned. Use the furrow to irrigate your crop and make harvesting easier.

If space is limited, you can plant potatoes in tyres or log beds. Add new tyres or extra logs with a further dressing of soil each time the stems elongate.

New potatoes are ready to harvest when the flowers are fully open, about 12 weeks after planting, and the tubers are about the size of hen eggs.

In Australia, the term 'bandicooting' refers to scrabbling about under the plants to gather just enough food for a meal, just as the native namesake does. Unlike this animal, however, you can investigate without destroying the root connections and leave undersized tubers alone to fatten up later.

If you leave potatoes longer, they develop their familiar hard skins and so can be stored. Harvest when the foliage has browned. Lift gently with a fork or with your hands to avoid damage. Shake off the soil and dry for a few hours out of the sunlight. Give them a rumble to remove excess soil, then store in an airy basket, hessian bag or a box in the dark, away from pests.

preserving the crop

STORING	Potatoes should be stored in a cool, dark, airy place. Remove "eyes" as they appear, and the life of your potatoes will be extended. Refrigerating potatoes converts the starches to sugar, causing them to become sweet. Direct sunlight produces a green skin – these potatoes should not be eaten.
FREEZING	Fresh potatoes are not suitable for freezing.

for the table

to prepare

• A common mistake is to boil potatoes covered. This results in a messy stove-top. Instead, just cover potato pieces with water, bring to the boil and cook, uncovered, for 10-15 minutes or until soft.

• Potatoes cook perfectly in the microwave. When cooking whole, pierce the skins all over with a fork, dampen the potatoes, cover with microwave-safe plastic wrap and cook in 5-minute intervals until soft when tested with a skewer. Potatoes pieces need a shorter cooking time.

to serve

• Wedges don't have to mean high fat. Place peeled potatoes in a pan of cold water and bring to the boil; remove from the heat and let stand for 5 minutes. Drain and cool until they can be handled. Cut each potato into 6-8 wedges. Place 2-3 tablespoons of vegetable oil in a bowl, add the wedges and rub all over with oil. Place the wedges on a large baking tray, sprinkle with sea salt and chopped herbs, if you like. Bake in a 200°C/180°C fan oven for about 30 minutes or until the wedges are starting to crisp. Turn only once.

• The secret to the perfect chip is frying them twice and sprinkling with salt as soon as they leave the oil – not 5 minutes later. Dry potatoes on a clean tea-towel or paper towel before frying and always use hot, clean oil.

• For delicious, creamy mashed potatoes, peel and cut potatoes into small pieces. Cover with cold milk. Bring to the boil and cook until soft but not falling apart. Drain, reserving any milk, then mash in the same pan, adding the reserved milk and a little butter.

• The creamy texture of boiled baby new potatoes, with just a sprinkle of sea salt, is loved by all.

• Try grated potato cakes with smoked salmon, sour cream and dill accompanied with a glass of chilled champagne for a delicious indulgent brunch.

• The Irish love their potatoes and colcannon is a traditional favourite. Boil 1kg potatoes until tender and mash with ⅓ cup hot cream and 40g soft butter. Melt 40g butter in large frying pan and cook 2 finely chopped onions and 1 crushed garlic clove until soft. Add 350g savoy cabbage and cook, stirring, until cabbage just wilts. Fold potato mixture into cabbage mixture.

• Potatoes carry the flavourings of the ingredients they're cooked with; they can extend a meal and make tasty snacks, lunches and breakfasts. Try adding any of these flavours to a plain mashed potato:

roasted garlic
sun-dried tomato pesto
basil pesto
bottled apple sauce (goes great
   with roast pork).

baby new potatoes

'Kipfler' potatoes

'Desiree' potatoes

'Sebago' potatoes

vichyssoise

50g butter

2 medium leeks (700g), trimmed, sliced thinly

750g coliban potatoes, peeled, chopped coarsely

2 cups (500ml) chicken stock

2 cups (500ml) water

300ml pouring cream

2 tablespoons coarsely chopped fresh chives

1 Melt butter in large saucepan; cook leek, covered, stirring occasionally, about 20 minutes or until softened (do not allow leek to brown).

2 Add potato, stock and the water to pan; bring to the boil. Simmer, covered, until potato is tender.

3 Cool 10 minutes, then blend or process soup, in batches, until smooth; place soup in large bowl. Stir in cream; cover, refrigerate 3 hours or overnight.

4 Divide soup into serving bowls; sprinkle with chives just before serving.

prep + cook time 1 hour (+ refrigeration) **serves** 6

notes Vichyssoise is the classic French creamy potato and leek soup that is generally served cold. You can also use 'Desiree' or 'Pink Fir Apple' potatoes for this recipe.

herbed baby potatoes

1kg baby new potatoes, unpeeled

1 tablespoon olive oil

60g butter

2 cloves garlic, crushed

2 tablespoons fresh herbs, such as rosemary, tarragon, thyme or sage, chopped finely (see notes)

1 Place potatoes in large pan, cover with cold water; bring to the boil. Remove from heat and stand in hot water 5 minutes; drain. When cool enough to handle, cut each potato in half.

2 Heat oil and butter in large frying pan; add potato, cut-side down. Cover; cook over medium-high heat 10 minutes or until the surface is golden and crisp.

3 Add garlic to potatoes in pan; cook a further 5 minutes. Sprinkle herbs over potato; toss gently. Season with cracked black pepper and sea salt.

prep + cook time 35 minutes **serves** 4-6

notes Choose the herb to suit the meal, e.g. sage with pork, rosemary with lamb, etc.
Serve hot as a side dish or at room temperature as a salad. The potatoes will be more crisp if served hot.

onions

Onions are one of the most widely used vegetables. For the gardening cook, to grow your own seems an impossible task, for to be self-sufficient in onions you'd need a small farm. However, unusual and special-purpose onions are worth the effort and the little space they require in a kitchen garden. They are easy to grow, and you'll have some bunching varieties for life. Onions store well in dry conditions and tiny onions are easily pickled.

in the garden

The soil for all bulb crops needs to be light and well dug so the roots can penetrate. It must also be well drained to prevent rot. If there are any hard clay clods, dig in coarse sand and fine organic material to open it up; mix it in well.

Should you have a hard clay base near the surface, raise the bed by mounding it over with garden mix or very fine compost. Sprinkle blood and bone or a complete fertiliser over the surface and rake it in. Make shallow furrows 0.5cm (¼") deep and sprinkle in the seeds. Cover with compost or seed-raising mixture and water well. If planting seedlings, place 10cm (4") apart.

bulb onions

To grow onions that develop into bulbs, you need to select the appropriate seed. 'Early' or winter-growing onions are sown at the start of autumn to give you white spring onions in spring. These can be pickled and used in dishes requiring whole small onions.

'Mid' and 'late' season onions are planted in mid-autumn or late autumn and are harvested in summer after their leaves dry out. Varieties include white, red and brown onions. These slow-maturers, after drying in the sun, are the best for storage.

green onions

Green onions (also known as scallions or bunching onions) can be planted all year round in really warm climates, but in the UK with its harsh winters you will need to avoid mid-winter. Buy seeds specific to this crop. They can be harvested in 8-12 weeks. For continuous supplies, replant every 4-6 weeks.

Here is a cheat's technique for cultivating green onions. When a recipe calls for green onions and you've bought a bunch, you'll probably have some left over; trim their stems by half and plant as a bunch, just covering the roots. They'll keep growing and be waiting for the next time you need some. They certainly won't turn into those soggy disappointments you find in the bottom of the fridge.

golden (or French) shallots

These are expensive and can be difficult to buy. Small bulbs can be grown at home from seeds, but are more often bought as sets or a bulb cluster. The bulbs are separated and pushed 5-7cm (2-3") deep into the soil, 15cm (6") apart in autumn or early winter. They'll multiply rapidly and you'll be able to harvest them in 3-4 months. Store in a dry place and keep enough for next season's planting. They don't appreciate very wet or humid conditions.

unusual varieties

• Potato onions, like golden shallots, expand their clusters of bulblets underground after planting in autumn. The bulbs expand as well as multiply. Harvest in spring or summer before the humidity rots them.

preserving the crop

STORING	Brown and white onions should be stored in a cool, dark, airy place. Red onions and the sweeter yellow onions store for longer in the refrigerator. Spring onions and green onions should be trimmed as little as possible and stored, wrapped in a damp tea towel, in a plastic bag in the refrigerator. Ideally, use straight from the garden. Bought green onions can be planted in the garden or even a pot until they are needed; they last for months and there is no waste.
FREEZING	Onions from the garden can be peeled, chopped and frozen for up to 3 months (see Freezing, page 113) in well-sealed plastic bags. Small onions can be frozen whole if peeled and blanched. Seal well so they don't spoil other food in the freezer. Onions can be gently fried, with or without garlic, and frozen for up to a month to give you a head start for busy, mid-week dinners.
PICKLING	To pickle small onions or shallots, salt peeled onions overnight, rinse and pack into sterilised glass jars (see Bottling, page 114), adding a few spices such as cloves, peppercorns and dried chillies as you go. Pour over warmed vinegar (malt, white or cider) to cover. For sweeter pickled onions, dissolve ½ cup (110g) white sugar in 4 cups (1 litre) of vinegar. Seal the jars and store in a cool, dark place for 3-4 weeks before opening.

spanish or red onions

spring onions

green onions

• Tree or Egyptian onions grow from bulbs planted in autumn and multiply underground. They also produce many small onions at the top of the flower stalks. If not gathered, these weigh down the stem until it touches the ground where they root and start a new cluster.

• Welsh (or, more correctly, Japanese) bunching onions are also called 'ever-ready' onions and are perhaps the most useful small onions of all. In a sunny, well-drained spot they will remain evergreen throughout the year and the leaves and stems can be cut and used like chives or green onions. To harvest, break off what you require and push the soil back around the clump. If the clump is too tightly packed, lift it with a fork, break off the excess and replant. The cluster will keep expanding, and will need dividing every couple of years to provide new space and soil to grow.

for the table

to prepare

• The biggest problem with onions, as we all know, is that they make our eyes water. Various remedies have been proposed: wearing goggles, holding a spoon in your mouth, only chopping onions on the full moon after midnight. The only tried and true way to avoid weeping is to get someone else to cut onions for you. So, the next time guests ask if they can help...

• For a dish where the size of the onion pieces doesn't matter (such as stuffing for poultry), use a food processor. It's quicker and prevents tears.

• When cooking onions with a roast dinner, cut in half and thread the un-cut sides onto skewers. They will be easy to turn and the centres won't pop out.

to serve

• For perfect barbecued onions, slice them thickly, put them in a heatproof bowl and pour over enough boiling water to cover. Stand about 15 minutes, drain and pat dry, then toss them in some vegetable oil and cook as usual. They can be prepared several hours ahead, covered and stored at room temperature.

• Sliced onion and tomato salad, drizzled with cider vinegar and olive oil, sprinkled with sugar and left to stand for about 30 minutes is also an old favourite. Try adding watermelon with a few olives and a sprinkle of chopped fresh parsley.

• This onion sauce is easy, can be prepared ahead, and goes well with grilled, roast or pan-fried pork. Heat some olive oil in a heavy-based pan; add some sliced onions, cover and reduce the heat to low, cook about 20 minutes, stirring occasionally. When very soft and golden add peeled, sliced apples, several crushed juniper berries, apple juice and a splash of gin. Cook, uncovered, about 15 minutes or until the apples are soft and most of the liquid has evaporated. This sauce keeps well, covered, in the refrigerator for several days, or can be frozen for up to a month.

• Glazed golden shallots are a great accompaniment. Cook peeled shallots and some crushed garlic in a little oil, covered, over low heat about 20 minutes or until very soft. Remove the lid and add some stock; bring to the boil and boil, uncovered, until the stock has almost evaporated. Add some sugar to the stock for sweeter glazed onions, if you prefer. Serve with any type of roast meat.

• Make a quick Thai salad using finely shredded red onions, whole mint leaves and wedges of plum tomatoes. Dress with a mixture of fish sauce, lime juice and a touch of sugar. Add some shredded cooked chicken, rare roast beef or flaked poached fish to make a main course. Add some chillies for a hotter version.

onion tart

This pastry is very easy and good for any savoury tart, but you can also use frozen ready-rolled pastry sheets, joined with a little egg yolk.

1 tablespoon olive oil

30g butter

5 large brown onions (1kg), halved, sliced thinly

3 teaspoons fresh thyme leaves

4 cloves garlic, crushed

¼ cup (40g) finely chopped seeded black olives

1½ cups (225g) plain flour

60g butter, extra

2 tablespoons grated Parmesan cheese

125g cream cheese

1 egg

1-2 tablespoons lemon juice, approximately

150g goat's-milk cheese

1 Heat oil and butter in large heavy-based frying pan. Add onions; cook, covered, over medium heat, about 5 minutes or until onions are softened. Uncover; cook, stirring occasionally, about 20 minutes or until onions are golden brown. Stir in thyme, garlic and olives; cook a further 10 minutes. Cool to room temperature.

2 Preheat fan oven to 200°C/180°C. Lightly oil 23cm (9") loose-based flan tin.

3 Process flour, butter, Parmesan and half the cream cheese until combined. Add egg and enough juice to make ingredients cling together. Roll dough on floured surface until large enough to cover base and side of tin; lift pastry into tin, gently ease into side, trim edge. Place tin on oven tray; line pastry with baking paper, fill with dried beans or rice. Bake 10 minutes. Remove paper and beans; bake a further 10 minutes or until pastry is browned lightly, cool. Reduce oven temperature to 180°C/160°C.

4 Spread combined goat's cheese and remaining cream cheese over pastry shell. Top with onion mixture; bake in oven about 30 minutes or until filling is firm. Serve at room temperature.

prep + cook time 1 hour 35 minutes (+ cooling) **serves** 6

note This tart will keep well, removed from the tin and covered, in the refrigerator for several days. Serve at room temperature.

broad beans

Broad beans are the first beans of the season and have a delightful shape. Their brilliant green colour, revealed by peeling, is irresistible, and their robust and earthy flavour makes them a treat to serve. For the gardening cook, a springtime crop of broad beans requires pre-winter planning, but the sound of bees in their flowers and their elegant grey-green foliage makes broad beans one of the chief delights of the spring kitchen garden.

in the garden

Broad beans are most productive in spring after surviving the cold of winter. Plant in autumn to winter in most climates, but not when the soil is very cold in frost-prone areas. The plants themselves do not mind frost, but the seeds won't germinate in these conditions.

There are two varieties of broad beans: one grows 2m (6') tall and a dwarf form reaches 1m (3'). Choose a site that enjoys winter sun, dig it over, distribute blood and bone, and water well. Press seeds 5cm (2") into the soil 15-20cm (6-8") apart. Sow in rows running north-south for maximum exposure to the sun, or in circular clusters. Shoots will appear in about 2 weeks. Water once then, without too much bother except the occasional watering, the bean plants will start to grow, but very slowly compared with summer crops.

The plants will need support as the stems grow tall and soft and will become top-heavy with beans in spring. Place a strong stake at each corner of your patch or at intervals around the cluster and attach rounds of twine. Make the first round at 30cm (12") high and another at 80cm (30") when needed. Carefully tuck lanky stems into the enclosure.

White and black flowers appear as the weather warms, and bees start to visit. Tiny black beans with a flag of withered blossoms means the crop is under way, some 18-20 weeks after planting.

The pods can be harvested while still pliable before the beans have hardened. At this stage they can be cooked and eaten whole. Otherwise, let the beans swell in the pods before picking. Carefully press the pods with your fingers to assess how large the beans are.

Any beans that escape your spring harvesting will be found later, dried on the plants. Store for use next season or, if not mouldy, store as dried beans.

An alert: some people of Mediterranean origin are allergic to broad beans.

for the table

to prepare

• Very young broad beans can be eaten pods and all but, generally, the pods are harvested later and only the podded beans are eaten. Cook in plenty of boiling water without a lid.

to serve

• Broad beans complement tomato-based lamb dishes particularly well.

• Add cooked, peeled broad beans to casseroles at the last minute; they add great flavour.

• For a broad bean dip, cook beans well, peel and puree with a little lemon juice, sour cream, ground cumin and lots of fresh herbs. Press plastic wrap onto the surface of the dip to prevent discolouring.

• Combine cooked, peeled broad beans and asparagus in a herbed vinaigrette.

preserving the crop

STORING	Do not remove the beans from their pods until you are ready to cook them. Store broad beans in the refrigerator for up to a week.
FREEZING	If blanched, without their pods, broad beans can be frozen for up to 6 months (see Freezing, page 113).

spring herbs

Throughout winter, the hardier members of the herb set will have survived to keep our food tasty and seasonal. Come spring, tender perennials like chives, tarragon and mint re-emerge and we discover self-sown seedlings of dill, basil, borage, parsley, coriander or nasturtium popping up. Most herbs grow well in pots and can be handy to the kitchen, but remember to feed and water regularly.

in the garden

parsley

Hopefully, parsley will have stayed productive through winter, in stunted form if your winter is very cool, but come the warmth of spring and longer daylight hours, the stems elongate and thicken. Parsley is a biennial plant (that is, it has a 2-year life cycle) and if you planted your parsley 2 years ago, it will probably start to seed this year.

To start new supplies, sow seeds through the warm months in punnets, pots or in the ground. Soak the seeds overnight to speed up germination.

If you let parsley go to seed, in no time you'll have tall, green, flowery tops and the many seeds will settle throughout your garden and provide you with copious new plants. It's said you have to be particularly wicked to get returns of parsley, but perhaps what should be said is that you're very lucky.

chives

Chives are small-growing, well-behaved members of the onion family, with a subtle onion flavour. The grassy clumps stand 30cm (12") tall and have pink–mauve flowers in spring. Chives are equally happy grown in pots, garden clumps or as border plants. They like a sunny, well-drained spot but can also cope with shade.

Don't attempt to grow chives in soggy conditions. They can be grown from seed or divided from a larger clump; otherwise buy a small pot from your nursery for an instant usable addition to your garden.

Soil should be richly manured. Liquid fertiliser should be given at least every month as you are growing a leafy plant. When the tips start to yellow, you know extra nourishment is needed.

As cool weather approaches, the leaves will die down. Remember to mark the spot to avoid disturbing the clump during winter gardening. In spring the chives will re-emerge. They can then be lifted and divided. This strengthens cluster bulbs.

Garlic chives have strappy leaves, longer than traditional chives, and white flower clusters. The furled buds are used in Chinese stir-fries. These chives also have an excellent garlic flavour and don't scent the breath, hence their occasional name, 'society garlic'. They like the same conditions and grow in the same manner as normal chives. Wild garlic, *Tulbaghia violacea*, can be also used in the same way.

chervil

Chervil is an unusual herb because it grows happily in shade – not deep shade, but filtered sun is preferred. It is also happy in a large pot, making it very convenient for small city gardens. In both gardens and pots, chervil needs to be kept moist.

Chervil is fern-like both in its appearance and growth. In good

preserving the crop

STORING	Herbs are best used straight from the garden, but can be wrapped in damp paper towel and stored in a vegetable storage bag in the refrigerator for several days. The flavour won't be as good so be generous when using.
FREEZING	All these spring herbs can be frozen (see Freezing, page 113). Coriander roots can also be frozen.
DRYING	Parsley, chervil and tarragon can all be dried successfully (see Drying, page 115) as can the flowers of chives and tarragon. Coriander loses its flavour when dried. Store coriander seeds in an airtight container in a cool, dark, dry place.

conditions it will grow for about 18 months before running to flower and seed. Gather some seeds and plant immediately. (If it's mid-winter, wait until spring.) Its leaves are fine, so harvest gently with scissors to avoid accidentally pulling out the plant.

tarragon

Tarragon, or *Artemesia dracunculus*, is a tender, delicately flavoured perennial sometimes called the 'king of herbs'. Seek out French tarragon in preference to Russian tarragon as the flavour is superior.

Ask a neighbour for some newly emerging offshoots (there will be an abundance) or buy a pot in spring. Plant in a spot at least 1 square metre (1 square yard) in full sun in soil that has been well manured with blood and bone or a pelleted slow-release fertiliser. Water well until established. Tarragon multiplies like mint, so keep your spade handy to control the spread.

coriander

This herb, essential in Asian cooking, is a parsley-like annual (often called Chinese parsley). The thing to remember is coriander prefers to burgeon when the weather is cooler (spring, autumn and even through mild winters).

Coriander's worst characteristic is running to seed, particularly in summer when it sometimes bolts. Just when you've got a row of seedlings up, or planted out seedlings into a sunny spot, they suddenly change leaf shape to develop fern-like foliage and a

flower on top. Save the seeds as they can be ground or used whole in cooking, or store them for future planting.

To avoid premature seeding, try planting during cooler conditions and adding massive doses of nitrogen to extend its growing time. Snip off leaves as required. This will thicken the plant. Pull out whole plants when bunches or roots are needed. This will thin the row or cluster and allows the remaining plants to grow more robust.

Vietnamese mint, which grows all through summer and all year in frost-free areas, is a reasonable flavour substitute for coriander.

for the table

to serve

• The classic French herb blend known as *fines herbes*, is a blend of fresh tarragon, parsley, chives and chervil; this blend is particularly good in egg dishes, sauces, salads and soups.

• Toss the whole leaves of freshly harvested herbs through salads for an instant flavour boost.

• Chervil has a delicate, slightly aniseed flavour and is used fresh in salads or sprinkled over vegetables. It goes well with egg, chicken and cheese dishes. Add a handful of chervil leaves to a gruyère soufflé.

• Tarragon is famous as a vinegar flavouring. Use a quality white wine vinegar and store for 1 month. New tarragon growth has the most flavour. Add fresh at the end of slow-cooked dishes as it becomes bitter if cooked.

• Roll a boned loin of pork or veal in chopped mixed spring herbs. Tarragon, chervil, parsley and chives are all good. Add some brown sugar and a few caraway seeds. Wrap tightly in plastic wrap and refrigerate overnight. Roast as normal.

• Parsley is full of vitamins and minerals, including iron. It aids digestion and keeps the kidneys healthy. The two varieties are virtually interchangeable but flat-leaf parsley tends to holds its flavour better and performs best in salads while curly-leaf parsley is best for garnishing. Add the stems of parsley to stocks (the leaves make the stock cloudy). Sprinkle gremolata (parsley, lemon rind and garlic) over rich casseroles such as lamb shanks and osso buco just before serving.

• Chives are delicate, so snip them with scissors rather than chopping with a knife, which will mince them. Chives add a slight onion flavour and are great in cheese and egg dishes as well as in salads and dips. The flowers are edible and look beautiful in salads.

• Coriander is an incredibly useful herb because every part of the plant is edible. It is essential to many Asian dishes and its pungent aroma is magical to many. Add the chopped leaves and ground seed to guacamole. The dried seeds are used whole or ground in both sweet and savoury dishes. Add the leaves and the chopped root to stir-fries and curries.

• Spark up your nachos with a tomato and fresh coriander salsa.

herb dip

125g cream cheese, chopped

½ cup (125g) sour cream

2 cloves garlic, crushed

1 tablespoon chopped fresh parsley

1 tablespoon chopped fresh tarragon

1 tablespoon chopped fresh chervil

1 tablespoon finely snipped fresh chives

tomato dip

2 medium tomatoes (380g), chopped finely

½ small red onion (50g), chopped finely

1 fresh small red Thai chilli, chopped finely

½ teaspoon ground coriander seed

1 tablespoon chopped fresh coriander leaves

1 Combine ingredients for herb dip in small bowl; mix well. Season to taste. Cover, refrigerate 2 hours; remove from refrigerator 10 minutes before serving.

2 Combine ingredients for tomato dip in small bowl.

3 Serve dips with coriander crisps (see opposite).

prep time 10 minutes (+ refrigeration) **serves** 6-8

notes Herb dip can be made up to a day ahead. Store, covered, in the refrigerator.
Tomato dip is best made close to serving.

coriander crisps

1 cup (150g) plain flour

¼ cup (35g) self-raising flour

1 teaspoon ground coriander

1 teaspoon ground cumin

60g butter

1 tablespoon lemon juice

¼ cup (60ml) water, approximately

1 egg white

1 tablespoon sea salt flakes

1 Preheat fan oven to 200°C/180°C.

2 Process flours, spices and butter until combined. Add juice and enough of the water to make ingredients cling together.

3 Roll dough on floured surface to 3mm thick; cut into triangles. Place on oiled oven trays. Brush with egg white; sprinkle with salt.

4 Bake about 10 minutes or until golden and crisp. Cool on wire racks.

prep + cook time 20 minutes **serves** 6-8

note Crisps can be stored in an airtight container for up to 2 weeks.

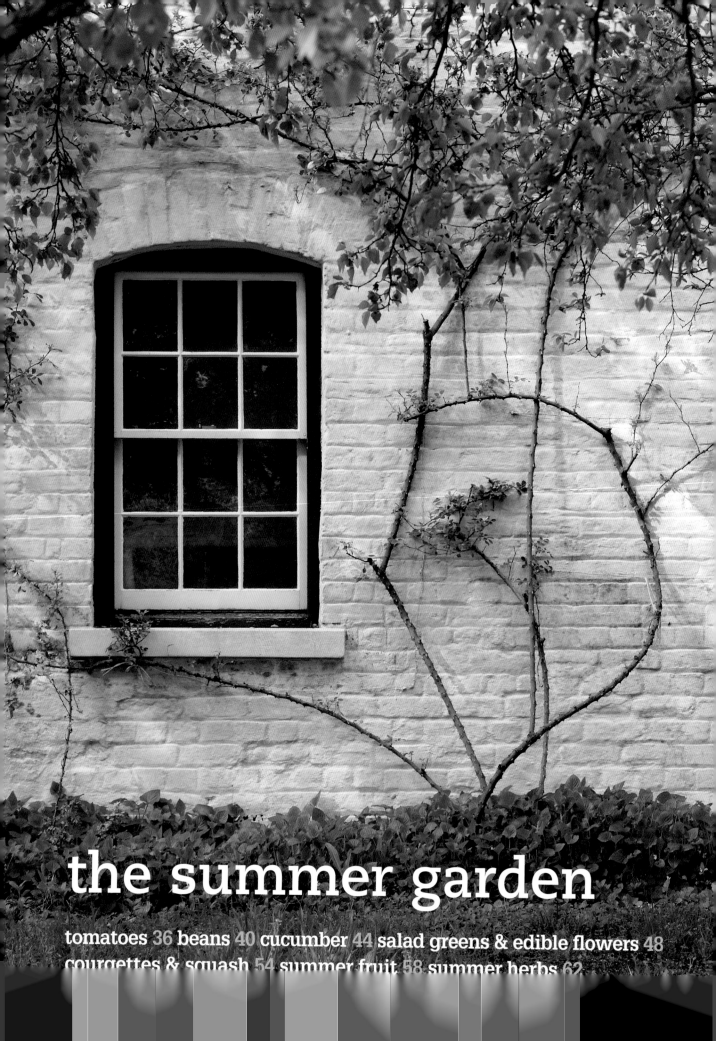

the summer garden

Water becomes scarce and your garden will almost certainly need your help to avoid drying out. Maintain a schedule of regular watering. Water in the cool of the day (early morning or late afternoon) to minimise evaporation and leaf burn.

Install a watering system, especially if you are planning a long holiday. Pots, in particular, dry out very quickly so need careful and constant moisture monitoring.

Spread mulch around beds to retain soil moisture and protect roots. Plant 'thirsty' plants together to make thorough watering easier. Irrigate with furrows between plants so that water goes directly to the roots. Avoid growing those plants that you find too demanding for your cultivating conditions.

Remember to take care of yourself. Don't work in the middle of the day and if gardening for long periods, wear a hat against the sun. Do only the essential maintenance tasks and leave the heavy garden jobs for autumn.

Most important of all, gather your harvest when it's at its peak. Enjoy the summertime treasures you and your garden have produced.

Don't let fruit or veg fall and lie on the ground – this encourages pests.

The heat is thick around us; it slows us down. The pace of living becomes languid, less urgent. A shady verandah invites us to sit, sip a long cool drink, to read, to sleep. We plan expeditions to the nearest watering hole. Long afternoon shadows are cast across the lawn. We come home from the beach sunburned and tired. Mad dogs and Englishmen ... it's just too hot to do anything.

Not so in the garden. Summer gardens don't slow down; they speed up. Everything grows like mad; leaves develop, fruits ripen overnight, vines unfurl before your eyes. The garden threatens to take over. Insects and diseases multiply to take advantage of the bounty. All your careful spring preparations pay dividends as summer fruits and vegetables burgeon around you.

sow now	harvest now
vegetables beetroot, broccoli, Brussels sprouts, spring cabbage, carrots, chard, courgettes, outdoor cucumber, endive, outdoor French beans, kale, lettuce, marrows, onions, peas, radishes, runner beans, swedes	vegetables asparagus, aubergines, beetroots, broad beans, broccoli, summer cabbage, carrots, cauliflowers, courgettes, cucumber, garlic, lettuce, melons, peas, peppers, early potatoes, radishes, runner beans, swedes, sweet corn
herbs basil, borage, chives, coriander, dill, fennel, parsley, sage, thyme	fruit apples, blackberries, blueberries, cherries, currants, figs, grapes, kiwi, peaches, plums, raspberries, strawberries

tomatoes

What's a summer vegetable garden without tomatoes? The first ripe tomato of the season is a guaranteed thrill for every gardener. It will probably only be enough for a single sandwich, but it will taste like ambrosia. What flavour! What perfume! As summer progresses, your tomatoes will swing into full production, and you'll harvest armfuls each evening – and wonder what to do with the sheer volume. Luckily, tomatoes are easy to preserve, and you'll be able to capture the rich, ripe aroma of summer. That is, until next summer when you once again await that first tomato.

in the garden

Tomatoes need well-drained soil with plenty of manure or compost dug in before planting. They also require the complete fertiliser of your choice, be it chemical or organic, to really develop well.

Tomatoes generally require full sun, and you should give them your warmest, sunniest position. Tomatoes cannot stand frost.

Nurseries sell seedlings, and grafted plants are available with disease-resistant rootstock. You can also buy seeds to raise in pots or trays indoors and in the greenhouse while frosts continue and the soil is cold. Seedlings take about 6 weeks to mature to transplantable size. If they develop too fast and the conditions aren't yet right, move the seedlings to 15-20cm (6-8") pots inside until the garden is ready.

'Ferline', 'Shirley' and 'Outdoor Girl' are among the popular, large-fruiting types. Plum-shaped tomatoes like 'Roma', are traditionally grown for preserving, drying and sauce-making as they are fleshy rather than juicy. There are assorted streaked and mottled tomato varieties, too.

The other main tomato variety is the small fruiters producing grape-like clusters in a range of shapes and colours. Some, such as 'Gardener's Delight', are slightly larger than bite-sized; others such as 'Sungold' and 'Sweet Million' are cherry-sized. These are the best for growing in pots. They will need a rich potting mix and regular watering and feeding.

Sow seed in spring in a propagator or warm windowsill in seed trays or small pots at 64°F. Transplant individually into small pots when two true leaves have formed. Plant your young plants outside after all risk of frost has passed into a prepared sunny position. Space them about 1m (3') apart, but if space is limited, they can be spaced at 50-60cm (20-24") intervals when staked. Hammer in strong stakes at planting time to avoid disturbing the roots later. Close planting requires regular watering and fertilising. Tomatoes develop large root systems, so give them as much space as you can.

Make furrows between the plants so the roots can be easily soaked. Avoid overhead hosing as it encourages leaf viruses and diseases. A good soaking with the hose every couple of days will keep tomatoes growing well. Poor watering is regularly the cause of poor flavour in tomatoes.

preserving the crop

STORING	Tomatoes are best stored at room temperature for up to a week. They can also be stored in the refrigerator for 3-4 weeks.
FREEZING	Tomatoes can be frozen, but they won't hold their shape when thawed, making them useful only in cooked dishes. The best way to freeze tomatoes is to peel, seed, chop and pack the pulp into small containers (see Freezing, page 113). Stir in chopped fresh basil for dishes that call for fresh herbs. Freeze for 6-8 months.
DRYING	For drying advice, see page 39; also see Drying, page 115.

roma or plum tomatoes

cherry tomatoes

kumato

Plants can be left to ramble naturally (they have a wide spread) or controlled on stakes by removing the side growths (from leaf axils) when they are about 3cm (1") long. Don't remove the differently-shaped flower spikes (you'll see the buds). Keep tying the plants to the stakes in loose figure-of-eight ties and break off the tip to halt growth when it reaches the top of the stake.

The flower stems will start to appear in 6-12 weeks and the fruit will form if there is good air movement to distribute the pollen and night temperatures are over 10°C (50°F). The tastiest fruit are those that ripen on the plant.

For outdoor cultivation, sow seeds around 8 weeks before the last local frost is expected and harden plants off for around 14 days before planting out. You will be restricted to outdoor varieties such as 'Outdoor Girl', 'Yellow Perfection' and 'Legend'.

pests and diseases

There is one disorder that all tomato growers fear, blight. This fungus turns the leaves brown, then the stems and then the fruit. Remove affected parts on sight and spray with a copper or mancozeb fungicide.

Pyrethrum-based sprays are a safe treatment for thrips, white fly and tomato caterpillar. There are also proprietary chemical treatments for the many fungal blights that tomatoes are heir to, but Bordeaux spray may be an alternative. Drop any infected or diseased fruit into hot water, burn it or seal in plastic bags to bake in the sun. Don't compost any fruit infected by fungal blights as the spores don't die in the process. Lastly, don't be put off by these warnings. Most gardeners raise terrific crops, and most tomato plants produce something, even in dire straits.

for the table

to prepare

For the best taste, leave tomatoes on the vine for as long as possible to allow their flavour to fully develop. When picked, store at room temperature. They will be much sweeter than those stored in the refrigerator as cold dulls their flavour. Tomatoes can last up to a week at room temperature in hot weather, and 3-4 weeks in the refrigerator.

to serve

• Barbecue tomato halves for a delicious smoky flavour.

• Cherry tomatoes wrapped in long thin slices of Lebanese cucumber, secured with a toothpick and served with pesto-flavoured mayonnaise make great summer finger food.

• Serve freshly sliced tomatoes, with a scattering of shredded fresh mint, ground black pepper and a drizzle of olive oil, as an accompaniment to easy summer dinners such as grilled fish, barbecued meats or chicken.

• For a quick lunch, toss halved teardrop and cherry tomatoes in a vinaigrette dressing. Serve on warm damper with fresh rocket and some strong cheddar cheese.

• A tip for school lunches – for non-soggy sandwiches, hold the tomato with the stem end up and slice through it to the base, not across the tomato.

• For a quick snack, butter toasted thickly sliced white bread; top with a thinly sliced ripe tomato, sprinkle with flakes of sea salt and a twist of ground pepper.

• Halve medium-sized tomatoes, put into a greased ovenproof dish and dot each with butter and sprinkle with salt and pepper. Bake, uncovered, in a moderate oven for 10 minutes. Serve baked tomatoes sprinkled with combined parsley and chopped shallots.

• Cut the tops off cherry tomatoes and scoop out some of the flesh. Beat some cream cheese and butter until smooth; add finely chopped basil, crushed garlic, mustard and some grated Parmesan. Pipe into tomatoes and chill until firm. Serve as finger food at a barbecue.

semi-dried tomatoes

Drying tomatoes

There are two methods: oven-drying and sun-drying. For either method, roma, or plum tomatoes, and cherry tomatoes have less juice and are therefore easier to dry (see also Drying, page 115).

Sun-drying needs good sun and low moisture. Place halved tomatoes, cut-side up, on wire racks in a deep baking dish and place in the sunniest possible position. Dry fresh thyme or oregano at the same time to add as extra flavour when bottling. Drying should take 3-4 days, the fruit becoming darker the longer it is dried. Bring indoors each night to avoid dew.

Oven-drying is faster. Prepare tomatoes on racks in oven trays, as above. Scatter thinly sliced cloves of garlic and oregano sprigs over the top. Cook in a very slow oven (100°C) for about 30 minutes, remove the oregano if completely dry and continue cooking tomatoes for another hour, then remove the garlic if crisp and dry. Reserve both herbs and garlic. Continue cooking tomato for a total of about 8 hours (5 hours for cherry tomatoes) or until they are quite dry (turn them several times while drying).

Pack tomatoes into hot sterilised jars (see Bottling, page 114), adding the dried garlic and oregano; completely cover with warmed, good-quality olive oil. Leave about 1cm (½") between the lid and the top of the oil. Store in a dark, cool, dry place for up to 8 months. Drain before using, but keep the oil for cooking as it will add a boost of tomato flavour.

Semi oven-dried tomatoes are cooked for 2 hours only. They are delicious tossed through salads with olives and balsamic vinegar. They have a much shorter shelf-life – about 5 days if stored, covered, in a little olive oil, in the refrigerator.

simple tomato sauce

⅓ cup (80ml) olive oil
4 small onions (320g), chopped finely
20 medium tomatoes (4kg)
8 cloves garlic, crushed
⅔ cup finely chopped fresh basil

1 Heat oil in large pan, add onions; cook, covered, over low heat, 20 minutes, stirring occasionally.

2 Meanwhile peel, seed and chop the tomatoes.

3 Add garlic to pan; cook, stirring occasionally, 5 minutes. Add tomatoes; bring to the boil. Reduce heat; simmer, uncovered, about 1½ hours or until mixture is the consistency of a pasta sauce. Stir in basil; cook, stirring occasionally, 10 minutes then season to taste with salt and pepper.

4 Pour sauce into freezer containers leaving 1-2cm (½-1") above sauce for expansion. Cover, cool in refrigerator, then freeze for up to 6 months or store in the refrigerator for up to 5 days.

prep + cook time 2 hours 30 minutes
makes about 7 cups

beans

Come summer the good vegetable garden is full of beans, in both senses. The garden comes alive with summertime produce and among the easiest to grow and most delightful of all garden crops is the bean family. Beans come in all shapes, colours and sizes; they grow anywhere in the sun, are perfect in small spaces and, best of all, are great to eat.

in the garden

Beans need well-manured and lightly limed soils and a frost-free summer. Plant seeds when the soil has warmed up and frosts have finished. Add a complete garden fertiliser. Beans also need sun and protection from wind.

Push seeds down to your second knuckle, or make a 3cm (1¼") deep furrow and drop them in 10-15cm (4-6") apart. Cover and they will emerge in about a week. A layer of compost, dried straw or leaf mulch will protect the roots, maintain soil moisture and suppress weeds. Beans require regular watering once the pods start to develop or they'll grow misshapen and stained.

Pick regularly when the pods are thin and the beans are tiny or fully formed. Detach the pods gently, preferably with scissors, to avoid snapping the stems. Should you miss some and the pods become wavy with enlarged seeds, pick and shell them and cook the seeds fresh. They will take about 20 minutes to soften and can be served on their own, added to sauces or served alongside whole beans.

After about 2 months the leaves will crinkle, lose colour and drop off. Cut off stems 10cm (4") above the soil and add all stem and leaf matter to the compost. Collect missed dried bean pods for next season's planting. Dig in the roots as they contain nitrogen.

You can also leave beans to dry on the vine until straw-coloured. Finish drying them under cover, then pod and store in an airtight container. While most bean varieties have white seeds, borlotti develop white and pink-streaked seeds, purple beans have pale green seeds and many climbers have brown seeds. Dried beans need to be soaked before cooking.

annual beans

These are planted each spring. They grow, flower and fruit through summer and then die down when the weather cools. Climbers will happily twist their way 2-3m (7-10') skyward over fences and walls, around lattice, stakes, tripods, netting, even wander up and over tall flowers and shrubs. Tripods can also be used in large pots if space is limited.

Dwarf beans grow to 50cm (20") tall. They form bushes, don't require support, and are good as borders. They are, however, not as productive as the climbing varieties.

runner beans

These are perennial beans and are good to grow where summers are cool. Their other name is 'seven-year beans' as they reshoot in spring for a number of years. They won't form pods if the summer is too hot. Pick the pods when only 15cm (6") long and before the seeds have swollen. If left on the vine, they become tough and the plant doesn't produce extra flowers and beans.

Both annual and runner beans come in all shapes, sizes and colours. Purple or yellow-podded types are available as well as red-, purple- or pink-flowered forms. Some pods are

preserving the crop

STORING	Beans are best picked as close to serving as possible. They can be stored in the refrigerator for a day or so, but never in plastic as they go mouldy rapidly.
FREEZING	All beans are suitable to freeze for up to 6 months. Blanch before freezing (see Freezing, page 113). Cook borlotti beans before freezing. Do not thaw beans before use. If adding to cooked dishes, add in the final stages.

borlotti beans

snake beans

yellow beans

flat and others are rounded; some have strings and others are stringless; some are short at about 12cm (5") long, while others, such as snake beans, reach 50cm (20"). The beans within can be the usual green, yellow, purple or streaked with red.

pests and diseases

White flies are a common pest. They suck the plant juices and weaken them, and can be seen hovering when the leaves are disturbed. Spray with proprietary insecticides bought for the purpose.

Leaf abnormalities include halo blight (halo spots on pale leaves), which is death to the plant (burn or seal leaves in plastic bags to dispose), and rust spots and powdery mildew, both of which can be treated with proprietary sprays. Read the label carefully and follow the manufacturer's instructions for usage.

for the table

to prepare

• Cook all fresh beans in boiling water, uncovered, for about 5 minutes or until just tender. (Purple beans turn green when cooked). For salads, remove early and cool in iced water.

• Microwave beans in a microwave-safe dish with a tablespoon of water, for 3-5 minutes on HIGH.

• Children enjoy snacking on beans fresh from the garden. Asking them to pick the beans can be a way of making sure they eat their greens.

to serve

• Toasted nuts make the perfect accompaniment to any bean. Toss beans in a little brown butter and add a sprinkling of nuts.

• Try beans with chopped basil, garlic and a squeeze of lemon juice (add juice at the last minute as it will discolour the beans).

• Combine beans with a tarragon-flavoured vinaigrette and serve warm or at room temperature.

• Toss some crispy pancetta, or bacon, and halved cherry tomatoes through just-cooked beans.

• Borlotti beans and tomatoes seem to be made for each other. Simmer them in *Simple Tomato Sauce* (see page 39) for a great vegetarian treat. Pan-fried pancetta can be added for meat-eaters.

• Snake beans, also known as 'yard-long', 'asparagus' or 'Chinese' beans, are long green beans similar in taste to green beans. They can be anywhere from 20-50cm (8-20") long, hence their pre-metric name of 'yard long' beans. They are great chopped into smaller lengths and used in stir-fries as they retain their crunch when cooked.

• Toss cooked green beans with slices of fresh tomatoes and red onion. Pour over combined soy sauce and sesame oil.

salade niçoise

200g baby green beans, trimmed

500g whole baby new potatoes

2 tablespoons olive oil

1 tablespoon lemon juice

2 tablespoons white wine vinegar

4 medium tomatoes (600g), cut into wedges

4 hard-boiled eggs, quartered

425g can tuna in springwater, drained, flaked

½ cup (80g) rinsed, drained caperberries

½ cup (60g) seeded small black olives

¼ cup firmly packed fresh flat-leaf parsley leaves

1 Boil, steam or microwave beans and potatoes, separately, until tender; drain. Rinse under cold water; drain. Cool, then halve the potatoes.

2 Whisk oil, juice and vinegar in large bowl; add beans, cooled potatoes and remaining ingredients, mix gently.

prep + cook time 30 minutes **serves** 4

prosciutto-wrapped bean bundles

200g green beans, trimmed

200g yellow beans, trimmed

8 slices prosciutto (90g)

60g butter

1 tablespoon rinsed, drained baby capers

1 tablespoon lemon juice

⅓ cup coarsely chopped fresh flat-leaf parsley

1 Cook beans in medium pan of boiling water until just tender. Rinse under cold water; drain. Divide beans into eight equal bundles.

2 Place one slice of prosciutto on board; top with one bundle of beans. Wrap prosciutto over beans; continue rolling to enclose beans tightly. Repeat with remaining prosciutto and beans.

3 Cook bean bundles in heated oiled large frying pan until prosciutto is crisp. Remove from pan; cover to keep warm.

4 Melt butter in same pan; cook capers, stirring, 1 minute. Stir in juice.

5 Serve bean bundles drizzled with caper mixture; sprinkle with parsley.

prep + cook time 30 minutes **serves** 8

cucumber

Cucumbers belong to a large family, the cucurbits, which includes squash, cucumbers, courgettes (zucchinis), marrows, pumpkins and melons. Like any worthwhile gathering of relatives, the family also includes some diverting members such as loofahs for the bath and gourds for decoration.

in the garden

Cucumbers are a true summer crop: they demand full sun and are killed by frosts. They also demand soil rich in organic matter (manure, compost, decomposed leaf litter). The more, the better. Sprinkle lime to reduce acidity, and a well-balanced garden fertiliser. Shape the soil into mounds 50cm (20") apart, creating a furrow around each to allow water to reach the roots easily. Push 3-4 seeds into the mounds just below the surface. For bush or compact varieties, halve this distance or plant them in pots 30-50cm (12-20") wide and deep and packed with a rich potting mix.

Seedlings will break through in a week or so, depending on the temperature of the soil. Reduce to the healthiest 2 plants per mound once the leaves have started to form. Turn the vines to grow in opposite directions. If growing indoors, grow pairs of seedlings in egg cartons or grow-pots so they can be planted later directly into the soil without disturbing the roots.

To save space, train cucumber vines up netting, wire, lattice or tripods where their tendrils support them. Another space-saving technique is to cut off the stem after several fruit have formed. Side shoots will form and flower.

Keep cucumbers very well watered while flowering and fruiting. Each plant carries both male and female flowers. Male flowers have a prominent pollen-laden stamen in the centre. Female flowers carry an embryo fruit behind each trumpet and the flower centre is rounded. In summer there are more male flowers than female; in spring and autumn there's an equality of sexes. Bees carry the pollen between the flowers, but if bees are in short supply, brush the pollen from a male flower onto several female flowers.

Cucumbers are best picked when small when their skins are soft and the flesh is juicy. Pick early and often, and more fruit will be produced.

Cucumber varieties are many and various. Elongated green cucumbers are perhaps the most commonly grown, but also available are the tiny pickling or gherkin types, the smooth-skinned Lebanese variety, ridged 'Burpee' cucumbers (10-20cm or 4-5") and the long 'Telegraph' and 'Burpless' (50cm or 20") varieties.

There's a green and white striped Chinese giant that reaches 1m (3') as well as round cucumber varieties such as the white-skinned apple or 'crystal' types. The West Indian gherkin has hooks all over its pale green skin.

pests and diseases

Cucumbers can be stricken by downy mildew that discolours and eventually kills the leaves. It usually appears at the end of summer and signals the end of the productive season. Proprietary sprays are available and provided they are within their use-by date these can be used, following the manufacturer's instructions on the packet carefully. Do not compost the diseased leaves but burn or wrap them up before putting into the rubbish.

Damping off is a condition where the stems of seedlings rot and the plants topple over.

preserving the crop

STORING	Don't wash cucumbers until ready to use. Store in the refrigerator in a vegetable storage bag for about 10 days. Once cut, wrap cucumber in plastic wrap and refrigerate for up to 5 days.
FREEZING	Due to their high water content, cucumbers are not suitable to freeze.
PICKLING	Make pickles from young cucumbers by slicing or cutting into quarters lengthways. Toss in a little salt and stand in a colander; cover, and place over a sink or bowl for 24 hours. Rinse thoroughly and pack into hot sterilised jars (see Bottling, page 114); pour over heated spiced vinegar (mustard seeds or dill seeds are good, with garlic and a few bay leaves) combined with a little sugar. Seal while hot and store in a dark, cool, dry place for 3 weeks before opening. These pickles keep for up to a year.

To combat it, do not plant the seedlings too deeply, make sure all organic matter is well rotted and don't overwater the plant in the early stages.

Leaves are often skeletonised by the larvae of the 28-spotted orange and black ladybird that grazes on the under-surface. These ladybirds are greenish-yellow with black spines and just over 0.5cm (¼") long. Crush them by hand or use a food-safe spray if there are fruit and bees about.

for the table

to prepare

• There's no need to peel cucumbers if they are picked young. If left longer, you can either peel them or run the tines of a fork along their length, breaking the skin as you go.

• To crisp ageing cucumbers, cut into thick slices, sprinkle with salt, place in a colander over a sink or large bowl; add some ice-cubes and cover. Stand for about an hour; rinse thoroughly in cold water and pat dry.

to serve

• The traditional cucumber sandwich is a must at all tea parties. They should be made on fresh bread (white or brown) using butter, not margarine. And, as all good hostesses know, the crusts should be removed.

• Make a warm or cold soup from pureed cucumber, well-flavoured chicken stock and a little cream. Add dill to garnish.

• Sauté cucumber in butter and add a sprinkle of green onions or chives.

• Cucumber cups filled with prawns in a Thai peanut sauce are a refreshing starter.

• Wrap smoked ocean trout or salmon around cucumber sticks with a thin spread of wasabi for Japanese-style finger food.

• Finely sliced cucumber tossed with mirin, chopped fresh dill and some horseradish cream makes a wonderful bed for char-grilled fish steaks.

• Make fresh Vietnamese spring rolls from matchstick-thin slices of cucumber, daikon, red pepper and carrots. Combine with soaked rice noodles and snow pea sprouts and wrap in rice paper rounds. Serve with a light soy and sesame oil dipping sauce. You can also add grilled chicken, fresh prawns or chunks of rare roast beef.

• Cucumbers are 95 per cent water, so are refreshing in salads. Use a vegetable peeler to shave long thin strips from a couple of carrots; place in a bowl with a thinly sliced cucumber, a couple of large handfuls of bean sprouts and some finely chopped fresh coriander. Toss with a lemon vinaigrette.

• Tzatziki is the traditional cucumber and yogurt dip from Greece. Combine yogurt, grated cucumber, a crushed garlic clove, a squeeze of lemon juice and some fresh mint in a bowl. This goes well with most meat dishes.

green cucumber

Lebanese cucumber

'Telegraph' cucumber

white or apple cucumber

chicken and cucumber salad

150g chicken breast fillet, sliced thinly

1 clove garlic, crushed

1 tablespoon lemon juice

1 teaspoon finely chopped fresh oregano

¼ teaspoon sweet paprika

2 slices wholemeal pitta bread (120g)

cooking-oil spray

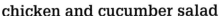

cucumber salad

1 telegraph cucumber (400g), halved lengthways,
sliced thinly

1 large green pepper (350g), sliced thinly

4 medium plum tomatoes (300g), seeded,
sliced thinly

1 tablespoon coarsely chopped fresh dill

1 tablespoon coarsely chopped fresh oregano

¼ cup (60ml) white wine vinegar

2 teaspoons white sugar

1 Combine chicken, garlic, juice, oregano and paprika
in medium bowl. Cover; refrigerate 30 minutes.

2 Toast bread; break into large pieces.

3 Spray heated medium frying pan with cooking-oil;
cook chicken in pan until cooked through.

4 Combine ingredients for cucumber salad in large
bowl. Add chicken and bread to salad; toss gently.
Serve immediately.

prep + cook time 25 minutes (+ refrigeration)
serves 4

chilled yogurt, cucumber & mint soup

3 medium green cucumbers (510g), peeled,
grated coarsely

1 clove garlic, quartered

1 tablespoon lemon juice

1 tablespoon coarsely chopped fresh mint

500g Greek-style yogurt

1 Place cucumber in sieve over medium bowl.
Cover; refrigerate 3 hours or overnight.

2 Reserve cucumber liquid in bowl; squeeze excess
liquid from cucumber.

3 Blend or process cucumber, garlic, juice and mint
until mixture is smooth; transfer to large bowl. Stir
in yogurt then add reserved cucumber liquid, a little
at a time, stirring, until soup is of desired consistency.

4 Divide soup among glasses; top with mint. Serve
with toasted Turkish bread, if you like.

prep time 10 minutes (+ refrigeration) **serves** 4

salad greens & edible flowers

No more does a salad consist of a lettuce leaf and a slice of tomato, nor is it the forgotten side dish. Today's salads are sophisticated combinations of leaf, flower, colour, shape and texture. Add an exotic dressing and tasty treats are yours in both summer and winter. Delicious to eat, salad greens make glorious decorative additions to the cook's garden. Grow them in pots, as borders and edges, or among the flower beds. A bed of lettuce makes an excellent filler crop in summer gardens, however, their delicate leaves won't survive late frosts. And be warned: in very warm conditions lettuce can run to seed easily and produce bitter leaves. There are 400 available varieties for just about every time of year, just remember to provide frost protection from late autumn to early spring.

in the garden

Lettuces must grow fast. They need rich, well-prepared soil. Spread a 10cm (4") layer of chicken manure over a sunny, well-drained site a month before planting, and cover with another layer of leaf, mushroom or well-matured garden compost. Dig all this into the soil at the end of the month.

Sprinkle seeds finely over the surface and rough up the soil to distribute. If planting in a seedling tray, cover with 0.5cm (¼") of seed-raising mixture or sand. Water lightly and the seeds will sprout in a week or less. Lettuce seeds will not germinate when the soil is over 30°C (85°F).

Thin tray-raised seedlings to 20-30cm (8-12") apart. Transplant these or purchased seedlings into the garden at the same spacings when their true leaves form. This is best done in the cool of the day when the sun has lowered. Water lightly but thoroughly.

Mulch well to keep weeds down and protect roots, but leave the stems clear to prevent fungal stem rot.

Lettuce needs regular watering and nitrogen-rich liquid fertiliser every 2 weeks. Lettuce can be grown in a heated glasshouse during winter in frosty zones.

types of lettuce

Crisphead lettuces are the most familiar of all the salad lettuces. They grow slower than other varieties and produce large leaves that curl inwards and enwrap each other to form a central ball. The leaves are light green and crisp, and remain cup-shaped when removed from their embrace, making them useful to use as containers in dishes such as sang choy bow. They also tear apart easily.

'Great Lakes' and 'Saladin' are two crisphead lettuces that won't bolt in warm weather. Butterheads are softer and looser. Harvest leaf by leaf until the heart has fully formed, then harvest it whole.

preserving the crop

STORING	Salad leaves and edible flowers are best picked as you need them – they keep much better in the garden. If you have to store them, wash salad leaves, not flowers, thoroughly in cold water, wrap in a damp clean tea towel and keep in the refrigerator for about 5 days at the most. Vegetable storage bags and lettuce keepers will extend their refrigerator life.
FREEZING	Salad leaves and edible flowers can't be frozen due to their high water content. The thawed-out sludge is of no use to anyone.
DRYING	Edible flowers can be dried (see Drying, page 115) but they will lose their flavour and colour, so use instead for pot pourri or non-culinary purposes.

rocket

baby cos lettuce

baby endive

'Cos' varieties grow tall and have tapering oval leaves that form a loose heart. These keep well in the fridge and are essential for Caesar salads. Semi-Cos are smaller, denser and sweeter.

loose-leaf lettuce

With these lettuces we see the full range of colour and texture possibilities, such as the softly frilled 'Salad Bowl', 'Lollo Rossa', 'Bijou', 'Frillice' and the neatly packed 'mignonette' varieties. There is even a red-leaved variety named 'Red Salad Bowl'.

salad greens

These are the more strongly flavoured leafy salad greens that enjoy the same growing conditions as the better-known lettuces but are in less demand. They are easy to grow in any garden as they take up little space, are ready to harvest in no time, and are fun to experiment with.

Rocket, also known as arugula, has a rich, peppery flavour. The leaves develop from the centre and are divided like dandelion leaves but have round edges. The surface is smooth and glossy. Rocket is easy to grow from seeds sown 10cm (4") apart. Cluster planting in a pot or garden is also useful, with further plantings each month. Avoid planting during the hottest months as rocket now earns its name and runs straight to seed. The leaves can be harvested leaf by leaf within a month. The plants will continue to thicken as long as they're well watered and fed. Pick off flower stems to stop early flowering but when replacements are growing, let a couple of plants bloom prettily, as they do, and collect the seeds for future plantings. With luck you'll find self-seeded volunteers all over the garden.

Mizuna, like rocket, prefers cooler conditions for generous leafy growth. The leaves are heavily dissected and almost fern-like in appearance and the pointed tips are soft. Its flavour is not as strong as rocket, but it does have its own almost grass-like taste. Leaves can be gathered in 20-30 days.

Radicchio comes in two guises. It can be lanky, loose-leafed and green with splashes of red, or tightly furled resembling a red cabbage. Both varieties have an almost bitter flavour. Radicchio combines well with other flavours but is often preferred on its own. Most green varieties re-sprout when cut 2.5cm (1") above the ground and develop into the red-hearted form in cool weather. Always keep radicchio well watered and fed.

Endive is grown in the coolest months. It, too, has a strong and sometimes bitter flavour. The more familiar loose-leafed frilly form requires regular water and mulching to prevent its roots from drying out and bitterness developing in the leaves. Gather a few leaves at a time while they are young, but to harvest the whole head, partially cover it with a plate or pot saucer for 3 weeks beforehand for a less bitter taste. Its blue flowers guarantee repeat crops as it self-seeds generously.

edible flowers

Edible flowers are the special province of the cook's garden. After all, one rarely buys flowers to eat, and your kitchen garden can yield a plentiful supply of unusual and striking blooms and petals to team with greens for a unique and individualised salad mix. Think of colourful nasturtiums, star-shaped borage, wonderful courgette flowers and the short-lived prettiness of day lilies.

butter lettuce

radicchio

cos lettuce

Wash all flowers very well and dry them gently. Take care when gathering blossoms that you don't harvest concealed bees as well. Make sure you have not used any pesticide or fungicide sprays, that your neighbour's sprays have not drifted into your garden, or that pets or birds have not left their marks.

So, what's safe to eat?

Calendula (*Calendula officinalis*) Its peppery orange or yellow petals are eaten raw in salads, on rice or in curries.

Chrysanthemum The petals are similar to calendula and can be used similarly.

Day lily (*Hemerocallis* varieties) These last only a day and colours include yellow, pink, cream, mauve and bronze. Pull off their green sepals and use the blooms whole or shredded in salads, batters or as garnishes.

Elderflower (*Sambucus nigra*) The small, white flowers form on a large head in spring, and the berries ripen to black in autumn. The flowers can be used to flavour champagne or to garnish punch; the berries are used to make wine and jellies.

Fruit blossoms (*Citrus, Malus, Prunus*) The petals of cherries, plums, peaches, apples, crab apples and all the citrus blossoms make lightly flavoured and pretty garnishes on cakes or sweet pies. Citrus flowers can also be crystallised or steeped in gin or vodka to make a citrus essence. Wash well to remove any chemical sprays and residues.

Geranium and pelargonium flowers and scented leaves Both can be used as garnishes on sweet or savoury dishes. The scented leaves release flavour when added during cooking: peppermint or citrus varieties are the most useful.

Grevillea flowers Often honey-laden, grevillea flowers make a exotic garnish and can be used to flavour ice-cream. Some leaves can cause a rash when handled so gather carefully.

Herb flowers Basil, parsley, mint, marjoram, chives and the like can be added as garnishes just before serving, but not during cooking. Blue borage flowers can be crystallised or frozen in ice-cubes to add a pretty touch to drinks.

Honeysuckle (*Lonicera* varieties) Remove the calyx and shred the petals of the sweetly perfumed varieties for a lightly honeyed, fragrant addition to ice-cream, milk desserts or icing.

Lavender The flowers of any scented lavender variety can be milled into sugar, added to ice-cream, biscuits or jams.

Marigolds (*Tagetes* varieties) These are the familiar, strongly aromatic group of flowers with bright yellow, orange or bronze petals. Their strong flavour and colour are used like calendula.

Nasturtiums Both the flowers and leaves are edible with a slight peppery taste and are good in salads.

Rose Loose petals and whole flowers can be used for garnishes, crystallised or steeped in honey (for a flavoured spread) or in alcohol (for rose essence). Roses are also used to make jams, jellies and other preserves. Dark-coloured blooms hold their colour best during cooking. Beware of bought roses as they are likely to have been sprayed with pesticides and other chemicals.

Vegetable flowers The blooms of peas, beans and seeding lettuce varieties can be added to salads.

iceberg lettuce

green oak lettuce

red oak lettuce

Male courgette and pumpkin flowers need to have their bitter stamen removed. They can be stuffed, then battered and fried. They can also be spread as a garnish on a quiche or frittata before baking.

Violet, viola and pansy flowers
Their velvet petals and deep colours look beautiful when crystallised, and also look good in salads.

for the table

to prepare

• At the risk of being repetitive, it is important to remember to pick edible flowers carefully, wash them thoroughly and to make certain that no chemical sprays have been used.

• Edible flowers, such as rose petals and violets, can be painted with beaten egg white and dipped in caster sugar for beautiful dessert decorations.

to serve

• The centres of firm, big-hearted lettuce can simply be quartered and then drizzled with a blue cheese dressing.

• The French make a light and tasty soup from shredded lettuce simmered in chicken stock with a little rice.

• Mizuna is elegant mixed with pear slices and enoki mushrooms, drizzled with a hazelnut oil vinaigrette and then sprinkled with chopped toasted hazelnuts.

• Try crisp prosciutto, teardrop tomatoes, prawns and rocket tossed in a spicy lime dressing.

• Add torn rocket leaves to pasta and toss with a chilli-tomato sauce.

• Chicken pieces marinated in red curry paste then barbecued or grilled are great served with mixed salad leaves, including mint. Add a squeeze of lime juice to finish.

• Mix soft lettuce leaves with rocket and a few peach slices. Serve with a berry vinaigrette.

• Halve radicchio heads, place in an ovenproof dish, add a slurp of olive oil and season. Cook in a hot oven (220°C/425°F) for 20 minutes, turning halfway through cooking. Serve hot or at room temperature with grilled meats.

• Make a bitter salad from shredded witloof, radicchio and radish; dress with an orange vinaigrette and serve with roasted meats such as pork or duck.

• Puree a mango with basil, lemon juice and olive oil, and use as a dressing over curly endive with edible yellow flower petals such as marigolds.

• Serve cos lettuce with a lemon pepper vinaigrette; add hard boiled eggs and shavings of Parmesan cheese.

• Toss torn baby cos leaves with thinly sliced, cored pears, roasted pine nuts and shaved Parmesan cheese; drizzle over a little olive oil and toss gently.

green salad with fennel & herbs

1 baby cos lettuce (180g), shredded finely

200g rocket, trimmed

100g watercress, trimmed

5 green onions, chopped finely

1 small fennel bulb (200g), sliced thinly

¼ cup coarsely chopped fresh dill

½ cup loosely packed fresh mint leaves

½ cup (80g) roasted pine nuts

red wine vinaigrette

¼ cup (60ml) olive oil

¼ cup (60ml) red wine vinegar

1 Place ingredients for red wine vinaigrette in screw-top jar; shake well.

2 Place salad ingredients in large bowl with vinaigrette; toss gently.

prep time 15 minutes **serves** 8

flower salad

250g mixed lettuce leaves

½ cup edible flowers or petals (see note)

raspberry vinaigrette

2 tablespoons raspberry vinegar

½ cup (125ml) light vegetable oil

1 Make raspberry vinaigrette.

2 Toss rinsed, dried leaves and flowers in large bowl; drizzle with vinaigrette. Season to taste.

raspberry vinaigrette Combine ingredients in screw-top jar; shake well. Season to taste.

prep time 5 minutes **serves** 6

note Experiment with a variety of seasonal flowers and greens. Mix mild greens with a garnish of stronger-tasting flowers and vice versa. Suggested flowers include violas, calendula, culinary herb flowers, pineapple sage, dianthus, day lilies and roses. If the flowers are large, use only their petals.

courgettes & squash

Courgettes, zucchinis to some, have the most delightful leaves: they are large, deep-green and robust-looking with very attractive white mottling. They may look lush, but don't grow courgettes too near your garden paths as the leaves are rough and brittle to brush against. Squash are a little more restrained in their growth habit and do not sprawl so wide. The flowers of both courgettes and squash are edible, as well as the fruit.

in the garden

Like cucumbers and other members of the cucurbit family, courgettes and squash require similar conditions: a frost-free growing time and full sun. They also demand soil rich in organic matter (manure, garden or spent mushroom compost or well-decomposed leaf litter). Add a complete fertiliser and lime to reduce acidity.

Wait until the soil has warmed and there is no threat of frost before planting. Shape the soil into mounds and push in 3-4 seeds to just below the surface. Both courgettes and squash ramble, so plant about 1m (3') apart to allow room to spread. Seedlings will emerge in 1-2 weeks. Once the leaves have formed, thin the cluster to the two healthiest seedlings and turn them to grow in opposite directions. They will ramble, but they are less leggy in full sun.

If established indoors, grow seedlings in egg cartons or grow-pots to plant directly into the soil when ready. They don't like their roots to be disturbed.

Keep courgettes and squash well-watered during the growing season. An irrigation soak is preferable to splashing the plants with a hand-held hose, and will reduce the possibility of mildew forming.

The flowers are bright yellow and trumpet-shaped. Each plant carries both male and female flowers. They start to appear in 6-8 weeks. Female flowers carry the embryo fruit behind each trumpet and have a rounded centre. The male flowers have only a stem behind and a prominent pollen-laden stamen in their centre.

Bees carry the pollen, but if they're not active, brush the pollen from a male flower onto the female centre to guarantee fruit formation. When there is an excess of male flowers, they can be gathered and eaten. Plants remain productive for 2-3 months.

courgettes

Courgette varieties come in various colours and shapes: cylinders of light green, dark green and yellow, balls of light green and dark green, and elongated straight and crooked-neck forms. Don't leave them on the vine for too long or they will become watery and their skins will harden. Pick when small because their flesh is juicy and their seeds are small. If your crop is abundant, remember that the male flowers can be eaten: remove the stamen, fill with stuffing and then batter and lightly fry.

squash

Squash vary in colour from bright green to yellow with green tops to variegated forms. All small varieties are interchangeable with courgettes in recipes.

Button squash are very popular and great for small gardens. Harvest when fully shaped but still small, otherwise their seeds and skins harden and the

preserving the crop

STORING	Store courgettes and squash in the crisper drawer of the refrigerator for up to 5 days. Do not wrap in plastic as this makes them sweat and go mouldy. Wash before using, not before storing.
FREEZING	Because of their high water content, courgettes and squash don't freeze well.
PICKLING	Slice thinly and brown quickly in a pan with garlic and fresh herbs (parsley and mint work well). Heat some tarragon vinegar with a little salt and a few peppercorns. Place warm courgettes into hot sterilised jars (see Bottling, page 114) and pour over warmed vinegar mixture. Seal immediately and store for a week before using. Great in antipasto platters.

blossom end rots. Compact squash varieties are well suited to pots.

Large white or green-skinned squash are available, as is the unusual spaghetti squash, which grows into a large melon with spaghetti-like stranded flesh. These larger varieties are picked when their skins harden.

pests and diseases

Like the whole cucurbit family, courgettes and squash are prey to mildew, which discolours their leaves and eventually kills the whole plant. It is caused by high humidity, rainfall or excessive watering. Proprietary sprays are available but check they are suitable for the crop and what interval to leave before eating. Do not compost diseased leaves; burn or wrap and place in the rubbish. Slugs will be tempted by young courgette plants and make light work of the crop. Use slug pellets sparingly or create a barrier around the plants.

for the table

to prepare

• Add both courgettes and squash to boiling water for a couple of minutes or steam until their colour is bright and they are just tender, about 5 minutes.

• Harvested when young, courgette flowers can be stuffed then deep-fried, oven-baked or steamed to make a delicious appetiser. The stem of the courgette is the baby courgette attached to the flower.

to serve

• Large white or green-skinned squash are always seeded, and can be sliced and steamed or stuffed with a meat mixture and baked slowly.

• For a delicious side dish, cook bacon in a pan with onion, garlic and butter until bacon is crisp and is onion soft. Cook squash until just tender; stir into bacon mixture and sprinkle with chopped chives.

• Cook squash until just tender, then toss in melted butter over low heat until coated.

• Cook spaghetti squash whole, then cut in half, pick out the seeds and add the spaghetti-like flesh to pasta sauces and casseroles.

• Fill courgette flowers with fetta, ricotta, basil and pine nuts, dip in a light batter and deep-fry in batches until the batter is crisp and golden.

• Stuff courgette flowers, with stems attached, with a mixture of ricotta and Parmesan cheeses, lemon rind and juice, some chopped mint and roasted pine nuts; twist the tops to enclose filling. Steam in a large bamboo steamer about 20 minutes or until courgette stems are tender.

• Bake hollowed-out courgette boats filled with minced lamb flavoured with yogurt and cumin for a healthy dinner.

• Cook finely chopped chorizo until heated through; remove from pan. Slice courgettes thinly lengthways and cook in pan until browned and tender. Stir chorizo through courgettes.

button or
patty-pan squash

yellow courgettes

green courgettes

courgettes flowers
with stems attached

char-grilled summer vegetables with herbed yogurt dressing

4 finger aubergines (240g)

2 medium courgettes (240g)

250g pumpkin

1 medium red pepper (200g)

1 medium yellow pepper (200g)

1 medium green pepper (200g)

¼ cup (60ml) olive oil

1 bunch rocket (120g)

herbed yogurt dressing

¾ cup (210g) reduced-fat yogurt

1 tablespoon snipped fresh chives

2 tablespoons chopped fresh parsley

1 tablespoon chopped fresh mint leaves

1 clove garlic, crushed

1 Make herbed yogurt dressing.

2 Cut aubergines, courgettes and pumpkin into 5mm (¼") thick slices. Cut pepper into 2cm (1") strips.

3 Brush vegetables with oil; cook on heated oiled grill pan (or grill or barbecue), turning once, until just soft. Layer vegetables with rocket; serve with herbed yogurt dressing.

herbed yogurt dressing Combine ingredients in small bowl; refrigerate until required.

prep + cook time 30 minutes
serves 6-8 as a side dish; 4 as a main course

summer squash salad

500g yellow patty-pan squash, halved

500g green patty-pan squash, halved

200g baby new potatoes, unpeeled, halved

⅓ cup (80ml) olive oil

2 tablespoons lemon juice

1 clove garlic, crushed

1 tablespoon finely chopped fresh dill

250g cherry tomatoes, halved

1 cup loosely packed fresh flat-leaf parsley leaves

1 Boil, steam or microwave squash and potatoes, separately, until tender; drain.

2 Combine warm squash and potatoes with remaining ingredients in large bowl.

prep + cook time 30 minutes **serves** 4

summer fruit

Fruit is superb in summer: richly coloured, plentiful and sweetly perfumed. With so many vegetables available all year round, summer fruits remain one of the few truly seasonal taste delights. We look forward to the shiny brightness of the first-season cherries, the wafting aroma of peaches, the dusty gleam of plums and the lush juiciness of gooseberries. Their delights are also fleeting. Summer fruits have a short season so harvest your garden's fruits with speed and dedication. Preserve, bottle, freeze or pickle your fruits to extend their perfection into winter.

in the garden

strawberries

These are in many ways a miracle crop, being the quickest fruit to crop after planting. In fact, with modern 'cold stored runners' you can enjoy strawberries just 60 days after planting.

Plants are short-lived however and tend to stay strong and healthy for around three years before needing replacement. The ability of strawberries to send out runners in summer compensates for this short life, and it's just a question of potting up some of the runners to make new plants to replace those that have become less productive. As a result, a strawberry bed may contain one-, two- and three-year old plants at various stages of life.

With their white and yellow flowers, and succulent red fruits, strawberries make pretty edging plants and are happy among herbs and flowers. There are many varieties to choose from which crop at different times of the summer: from earliest 'Emily' and 'Honeoye'; mid-season 'Pegasus' and 'Hapil'; and late 'Symphony' and 'Rhapsody'.

Buy virus-free plants during the summer and dig them into rich, free-draining soil. A straw mulch (hence the name 'straw' berry) protects them during winter, suppresses weeds and keeps the fruit clear of the soil. Modern gardeners tend to use a plastic mulch or even grow strawberries off the ground so that they aren't preyed on by slugs, and the fruits are protected from rain splash. Terracotta strawberry pots save space but need a lot of maintenance, in particular, watering and extra fertiliser to each pocket.

A strawberry plant's first summer is just about establishment. Cut off any runners and feed in late summer and autumn. Come spring, though, and the plants really get growing.

Slugs, snails and birds will also rush to the harvest. Pellets and traps will deter slugs and snails, and nets will help stop the birds.

Buy the time these plants reach three years old you should be thinking about replacements. Plant new runners in a new, well-prepared site and you'll get fruit the following year. Pull out old plants.

Alpine strawberries, despite their name, actually grow in most climates. The fruit is small but highly flavoured.

picking the crop

Pick the fruits keeping the stalk intact from mid-morning onwards when ripe and dry.

preserving the crop

STORING	Pick berries just before using. Net them to beat birds and squirrels and store in the refrigerator in a covered container lined with absorbent paper. Avoid washing. Strawberries last for about three days in the fridge.
FREEZING	Berries can be frozen as purees (see Freezing, page 113). The puree keeps, frozen, for up to a year.
PICKLING	We are all familiar with strawberry jam, but most berries contain only a small amount of pectin, which is needed to set jam. Spoon hot jams into hot sterilised jars and seal while hot (see Bottling, page 114).

blueberries

blackberries

raspberries

Berries

Berries thrive in areas with cool-to-cold winters, gentle springs and warm, sunny summers. Traditionally many berries had thorns but breeders have bred several thornless strains that reduce the risk of sharp scratches.

gooseberries

Dessert varieties surpass the less tasty culinary forms of these traditional woody plants, and cultivars such as 'Careless', 'London', 'Leveller' and 'Langley Gage' should be sought for green, red, yellow and white fruits respectively. For a thornless variety try 'Pax'. Plant new bushes in spring or autumn in well-prepared fertile soil around 1.5m (5ft) apart. Net the crop from spring onwards against fruit-stripping birds, and water well in summer to prevent stressing the plants. Gooseberries fruit on older wood and at the base of young wood. Prune after harvesting in late autumn to late winter, cutting new growth back to two buds and leaders back by a third.

raspberries

Nothing beats the taste of fresh raspberries and cream, and they make tasty addition to pies and muesli. They thrive in the British climate where are two types grown: bountiful summer-fruiting and late-fruiting autumn varieties. Summer varieties should be trained on two parallel wire supports, while autumn-fruiting varieties don't require support but can be planted between two posts and wires to keep them tidy. Summer-fruiting types crop on last year's canes, while autumn varieties crop on this year's.

Start a new patch in autumn with certified virus-free stock, planting canes around 30cm (12") apart in rows. Choose reliable croppers such as 'Glen Ample', 'Glen Moy' and 'Glen Prosen' (all summer) and 'Autumn Bliss' and 'Joan J' (both autumn-fruiting types). For abundant spring growth, mulch well every year adding plenty of well-rotted manure to the row. In autumn, after fruiting, cut out the dead canes and thin the rest to 5-6 canes each. Pull up any suckers in the row when they appear.

blackberries and 'friends'

These are vigorous unfussy trailing berries and, like raspberries, are thorny, although there are some thornless cultivars such as 'Oregon Thornless' which make pruning and picking less painful. Because they flower late they can be planted in frost pockets. 'Friends' include loganberries, boysenberries, tayberries and youngberries. Attach the trailing canes to a trellis and cut off at ground level after fruiting. Tie up each new cane as it develops. This will make the plant easy to harvest and stop it becoming a dense thicket.

blueberries

Blueberries grow on a thornless shrub that colours in autumn. The berries ripen from late summer into autumn. They need peaty, acid soil to do well, plus a cool-to-cold winter. You can grow them in pots with the right soil mix.

currants

Currants grow in grape-like clusters (red, black or white) on shrubs. Plant in autumn, winter or spring when plants are available from

red currants

nurseries. Give them a protective mulch in winter if the weather is very cold. Black currants fruit on new wood, so cut the stems back in winter to 10cm (4") above the soil. Red and white currants fruit on old stems, so prune only as needed to shape and control the shrubs. Each spring give all varieties a dressing of manure and a complete plant food, but keep clear of the stems. Repeat in late summer.

for the table

to serve

• Eat blueberries for breakfast picked off the bush.

• Raspberry jam that is baked rather than boiled is superbly flavoured.

• Berries make great-tasting, colourful vinegars for salads and sauces. Pour good-quality white wine vinegar over halved fruit and add cardamom pods or cinnamon sticks, if you like. Cover and stand for 2 days. Discard the fruit and spices and pour the flavoured vinegar into hot sterilised bottles (see Bottling, page 114). Store in the refrigerator for up to 1 year. The vinegar becomes sweeter as it ages.

• For a hot, sweet soufflé either place chopped fruit in the base of the dish or add pureed berries to a basic sweet soufflé mixture.

• A summer fruit platter is the perfect finish to a barbecue. Arrange slices of fresh peaches, apricots, plums, nectarines and strawberries on a large platter; drizzle over raspberry pulp and sprinkle with a variety of berries.

balsamic strawberries with mascarpone

500g strawberries, halved
¼ cup (55g) caster sugar
2 tablespoons balsamic vinegar
1 cup (250g) mascarpone cheese
1 tablespoon icing sugar
1 teaspoon vanilla extract
¼ cup coarsely chopped fresh mint

1 Combine strawberries, caster sugar and vinegar in medium bowl, cover; refrigerate 20 minutes.

2 Meanwhile, combine mascarpone, sifted icing sugar and extract in small bowl.

3 Stir mint into strawberry mixture; divide among serving dishes. Serve with mascarpone.

prep time 10 minutes (+ refrigeration) **serves** 4

note Standing the strawberries with the vinegar and sugar brings out their flavour.

summer herbs

Summertime is the very season for herbs. Almost every herb is romping by summer. There will be generous supplies in the garden or in pots within easy reach of the cook's kitchen. The two herbs featured, basil and mint, are at their most pungent and flavourful in the heat of the summer sun.

in the garden

basil

Basil is the 'queen' of the summer herbs. It originally came from India even though it is now synonymous with Mediterranean cuisine. Varieties are also used throughout Asia and are added to noodles, curries and soups.

Its strong scent evokes high summer and its lush, green leaves scattered over salads and pasta captures the essence of warm weather. Its leaves are also an honest indicator of the turn of the seasons as they start to blacken and wither in cool winds.

Basil is an annual herb, but you might be lucky to find self-sown seedlings in your garden from last year. Otherwise, pots, punnets and seeds are readily available from nurseries during spring and summer.

Plant seedlings in a sunny site in a rich garden bed or large pot after all frosts and cold winds have finished. If spaced 15-20cm (6-8") apart they will support each other as they grow.

Basil is lovely planted near a path or steps where you accidently brush the leaves at each passing. Pinch out the flower heads as they start to form, and gather sprigs by nipping back the top of the stem to a pair of leaves. This will thicken the plant.

Feed with a liquid fertiliser every 2 weeks, but spray late in the day to avoid leaf burn. Always wash the leaves before using. Slugs, grasshoppers, snails and caterpillars will want a share, but most pests can be seen and caught before they've done too much damage.

mint

Mint grows in most climates all year round, although in very cool areas it will need protective mulch during winter. But in summer mint really romps, growing tall, flowering and extending invasive new stems underground to take control of your herb bed.

The best form of control is confinement in pots or troughs. These can be dug into the garden with their rims above the soil, but watch out for stems that escape over the edge.

The scent of mint is delightful and there are a number of varieties – common garden mint with its mild flavour and rounded leaves, apple mint with its furry foliage, spearmint with its glossy pointed leaves, and peppermint with slightly purple-toned leaves. 'Eau-de-cologne' is named because of its perfume and, although not used in the kitchen, it's lovely to brush past.

preserving the crop

STORING	Pick herbs as close to using as possible. Basil, in particular, is very fragile and blackens easily. Store in a plastic bag wrapped loosely in absorbent paper towel for up to 3 days.
FREEZING	Both mint and basil can be frozen (see Freezing, page 113) for up to 6 months. Freeze sprigs in a rigid container and pluck off the frozen leaves as you need them. Once frozen, basil and mint are best used in cooked dishes. Another good idea is to chop basil finely, mix with butter and freeze as a log. Slice off a portion as you need it.
DRYING	Dried basil has not much flavour and has limited uses in the kitchen. Dried mint (see Drying, page 115) is used widely in teas, often mixed with chamomile.

Mint loves water and grows best with regular supplies; it will, however, recover if forgotten. Mint is much more aromatic if grown in full sun but it does tolerate partial shade. Flowers are mauve, cream or white. Give it a 'haircut' after it flowers.

Vietnamese mint or laksa herb grows in the same generous way as mint, but is not a mint at all. Its strong flavour is not dissimilar to coriander and it can be used as a substitute. It is, of course, added to laksas (noodle soup). Cut away the midrib if it gets woody and replace plants each spring.

for the table

to serve

• Basil is a must with tomatoes. Leaves are best torn, not cut. Scatter over tomatoes and drizzle with olive oil.

• Add basil to any dish. To fully enhance its flavour, stir in extra fresh leaves at the end of cooking.

• Basil pesto is justifiably famous. Stir into soups and stews at the last minute, or spread on crusty bread before toasting for bruschetta.

• A pizza base spread with pesto under the tomato base is delicious.

• Place whole basil leaves over the centre of a boned loin of pork, cover with seasoning, roll and roast. Also add basil to the gravy for extra flavour.

• A great dressing for a lamb salad is to puree basil with a green apple, garlic, lemon juice and oil.

• Mint cooked with apples makes a traditional mint jelly. Cook apples until they go rosy pink but don't strain the pulp through muslin or the result will be cloudy.

• For a mint sauce to serve with lamb, combine water, white wine vinegar and sugar in a saucepan and heat until sugar dissolves; pour over coarsely chop fresh mint leaves in a heatproof bowl and stand for 3 hours. Strain liquid into a bowl; discard mint. Chop more fresh mint and add to the liquid. Blend until chopped finely.

• Mint mixed with low-fat yogurt, garlic and seeded cucumber serves as a dip or a sauce over grilled fish or chicken.

• Wrap whole mint leaves, prawns and julienne vegetables in soaked rice paper rounds and serve with a lemon grass and mint sauce.

• Freeze mint leaves in ice-cubes and add to long cool drinks.

• Make a refreshing mint tea by pouring boiling water over freshly picked mint leaves; drain, reserving the mint. Combine the mint with more boiling water, some sugar and green tea in a saucepan, and stir over heat until the sugar dissolves. Bring to the boil then strain into a heatproof jug. Stir through more fresh mint and serve.

Vietnamese mint

common garden mint

sweet or common basil

purple basil

watermelon, mint and fetta salad

2 teaspoons white sugar

¼ cup (60ml) lime juice

½ cup (100g) crumbled fetta cheese

½ small red onion (50g), sliced thinly

½ cup coarsely chopped fresh mint

850g seedless watermelon, cut into wedges

1 Dissolve sugar in small jug with juice.

2 Combine juice in large bowl with cheese, onion and mint; spoon over watermelon.

prep time 10 minutes **serves** 4

notes Don't chop the mint until just before making this salad – it tends to blacken and go limp after it's been cut.
Use a fairly bland fetta so that its flavour doesn't overpower the melon.

basil pesto

2 cups firmly packed fresh basil leaves

2 cloves garlic, quartered

⅓ cup (50g) roasted pine nuts

½ cup (40g) coarsely grated Parmesan cheese

¾ cup (180ml) olive oil

1 Blend or process basil, garlic, nuts and cheese until chopped finely. With motor operating, gradually add oil in a thin, steady stream; process until smooth.

prep time 10 minutes **makes** 1 cup

note Pesto will keep, refrigerated, for up to one week; spoon into a screw-top jar and cover with a thin layer of olive oil. If you want to keep it longer, freeze in the same container. Pesto will never freeze solid because of its high oil content, so you can easily remove a little at a time.

the autumn garden

The delights of summer inevitably fade, but with autumn comes the best conditions for working in the garden, clearing up debris, straggling leftovers and dried remains that can all be composted when not diseased. If you have mountains of fallen leaves, pile them in a corner with handfuls of nitrogen-rich fertiliser, weigh them down with netting or a tarpaulin and leave them to mature for you to use as a summer mulch.

Days begin to shorten and the first signs of autumn start to appear. Mornings and evenings are just that bit cooler, and a warm spot in the sun is soon a sought-out pleasure. There's no denying the altered slant of the sun and the changes in the garden as plants prepare for the approach of winter, more spectacular in some parts of the world than others. Leaves begin to change colour and fall, and there's a sedate reduction, a battening down for the lean times of the winter ahead.

Plant out ready-prepared or bought seedlings to guarantee winter supplies. It is often a good idea to keep a record of what grew where in the garden over summer, what was successful, what caused more trouble than it was worth and what was not a treat to eat.

Deep digging and spreading around manure or compost to revitalise gardens becomes a pleasure in the cool weather. If you've got areas that are becoming shaded as the sun dips, leave them deeply mulched with manure and straw or grass clippings until the spring.

Prune shrubs and trees that block sunlight or lean over too far. Perennial vegetables like artichokes, chillies, peppers and asparagus benefit from pruning before being mulched for protection against frost. Check soil is well drained to stop root rot and stunted growth. Build up soil levels with mulch and compost.

Enjoy drying, preserving and storing your summer bounty.

pick now	plant now
most gardens apples, artichokes, broccoli, cabbage, carrots, chillies, early citrus, grapes, Jerusalem artichokes, kiwifruit, leeks, lettuce, melons, olives, pears, pumpkins, silver beet, spinach, and all summer crops still fruiting.	most gardens Asian greens, bay, spring cabbage, carrots, garlic, lettuce, mizuna, rhubarb, rocket, turnips.

globe artichokes

Who would believe that a thistle could look and taste so good? Globe artichokes belong to the thistle family, and are the flower buds of a wonderful grey-leafed plant that contributes a stunning architectural element to any flower-bed or vegetable patch. Subtle they are not; artichoke plants are tall and dramatic and require almost 1m (3') of space all round for their branches to spread.

in the garden

Provide artichokes with deep, well-manured soil and plant in spring in temperate climates or late autumn or winter in milder gardens. Well-rooted offshoots from an established plant may be available from friends or as plants from large nurseries. Artichokes are perennials, so once planted, they'll last 3-4 years. Treat them as annuals in frosty gardens by raising fresh seed indoors or under glass, and planting them out as soon as the frosts are over.

Give artichokes side dressings of complete garden fertiliser or pelleted poultry manure to ensure strong growth and buds at each branch end.

Cut the buds when they are still tightly closed and about 5-6cm (2-2½") round. Don't leave the globes on the plant too long as a dry thistle top will develop and other buds will not form once flowering begins. If you reduce the number of buds on the stems as soon as they start to develop, you'll force fewer, but larger, globes.

After flowering, keep artichokes watered, and in autumn cut the stems back to 30cm (12") above the soil. Spread a protective and nourishing mulch of well-composted manure around the plants for the winter and to give them a good start come spring.

for the table

to prepare

When preparing artichokes there's no need to snip off the top third of the leaves unless you are bothered by their tattiness or they are the variety with a small spike at the end of each leaf. Always remove the tough bottom leaves.

Rub cut surfaces with a lemon as artichokes discolour rapidly, or place in a bowl of lemon juice and water (acidulated water) until ready to use.

You may like to remove the choke. Pull the centre leaves apart and, using a teaspoon, dig out the hairy choke and some of the tiny inner leaves.

Boil, steam or microwave artichokes until just tender. Always cook artichokes in a non-reactive pan, or your artichokes will blacken.

preserving the crop

STORING	Although artichokes are best eaten soon after harvest, they can be stored, unwashed, in a vegetable storage bag in the refrigerator for up to 4 days. Wash just before using.
FREEZING	Artichoke hearts can be blanched and frozen (see Freezing, page 113). Break away the outside leaves and blanch hearts in acidulated water; drain well. Freeze for up to 4 months.
PICKLING	Artichoke hearts can be cooked in spiced vinegar and stored in olive oil (see Bottling, page 114) for about 3 months. Toss the cooked hearts in herbs before covering with olive oil.

to serve

• Most artichoke recipes call for dipping the leaves in sauces. The Italian sauce, bagna cauda, with anchovies, is great but Hollandaise goes just as well.

• Artichokes can be stuffed and baked. Try a mixture of breadcrumbs, pancetta and basil or oregano. Place stuffing between the artichoke leaves and bake. Drizzle with a flavoured mayonnaise and add a few anchovies for their salty taste.

• Add cooked and quartered artichokes to salads, especially Mediterranean ones. Add a touch of mint to the vinaigrette for a refreshing flavour.

• Top chicken fillets with cooked artichoke hearts, pour over cheese sauce, sprinkle with Parmesan and mozzarella and grill until golden and bubbling.

• Serve artichokes hearts on toasted focaccia bread. Drizzle with garlic oil.

• Toss cooked, quartered artichokes in combined oil, white wine vinegar and crushed garlic. Refrigerate, covered, about 3 hours, then combine with thinly sliced red onion and chopped oregano.

• Creamy sauces are great accompaniments to artichokes, especially a creamy mushroom sauce. Cook some sliced mushrooms and crushed garlic in butter and oil until soft. Add some white wine, wholegrain mustard, sour cream, cream, oregano, chives and chopped sun-dried tomatoes and simmer until the sauce thickens.

• A favourite dish in Italy accompanies artichokes with a lemon caper dressing. Drizzle hot artichokes with combined lemon juice, olive oil, crushed garlic, chopped capers and some chopped parsley.

• Do not discard the stem of young artichokes. About 15cm (6") is edible. Cook the heads, then peel and slice, and add to dishes in the final stages.

artichokes with lemon herb butter

80g butter, softened
2 teaspoons finely grated lemon rind
1 tablespoon finely chopped fresh flat-leaf parsley
2 teaspoons finely chopped fresh basil
4 medium globe artichokes (800g)

1 Combine butter, rind and herbs in small bowl. Place on piece of plastic wrap; shape into log, wrap tightly. Freeze until firm.

2 Meanwhile, remove and discard tough outer leaves from artichokes. Trim stems so artichoke bases sit flat.

3 Cook artichokes in large saucepan of boiling water about 40 minutes or until tender; drain.

4 Serve hot artichokes topped with slices of herb butter; accompany with lemon wedges.

prep + cook time 50 minutes (+ freezing) **serves** 4

artichoke hearts vinaigrette

1 medium lemon (140g), chopped coarsely

20 small globe artichokes (2kg)

2 cups (500ml) dry white wine

¼ cup loosely packed fresh thyme leaves

5 cloves garlic, unpeeled

½ cup (125ml) lemon juice

2 teaspoons sea salt flakes

1 cup (250ml) white wine vinegar

2 cups (500ml) water

1 tablespoon extra virgin olive oil

1 Place lemon in large bowl half-filled with water. Discard outer leaves from artichokes; cut tips from remaining leaves. Trim, then peel stalks; place artichokes in lemon water.

2 Cut a piece of baking paper into a round to fit inside a large saucepan.

3 Combine wine, thyme, garlic, juice, salt, vinegar, the water and drained artichokes in large pan; cover with baking-paper round. Bring to the boil; simmer, covered, about 25 minutes or until artichokes are tender. Cool in poaching liquid about 30 minutes.

4 Whisk ½ cup of the poaching liquid in small bowl with oil (discard remaining poaching liquid).

5 Halve artichokes lengthwise; remove chokes. Drizzle artichokes with poaching mixture to serve.

prep + cook time 1 hour 30 minutes (+ cooling) **serves** 4

artichokes with lemon pepper Hollandaise

1½ cups (375ml) water

1 cup (250ml) white wine

⅓ cup (80ml) olive oil

4 bay leaves

6 medium globe artichokes (1.2kg), trimmed

lemon pepper Hollandaise

3 egg yolks

2 teaspoons finely grated lemon rind

1½ tablespoons lemon juice

½ teaspoon cracked black pepper

250g unsalted butter

1 Combine water, wine, oil and bay leaves in large pan; bring to the boil. Add artichokes; simmer, covered, 30 minutes or until tender. Drain.

2 Meanwhile, make lemon pepper Hollandaise.

3 Halve artichokes lengthwise; remove chokes. Drizzle artichokes with Hollandaise to serve.

lemon pepper Hollandaise Blend egg yolks, rind, juice and pepper until combined. Melt butter in small pan until bubbling. With motor operating, add hot butter to egg yolk mixture in a thin steady stream; blend until mixture is thick and creamy.

prep + cook time 40 minutes **serves** 6

notes Artichokes can be prepared an hour ahead. Hollandaise is best made close to serving; avoid adding the milk residue from the butter to the mix.

carrots

Why bother growing carrots? They're cheap and plentiful in the supermarket, after all. Yet these colourful and familiar vegetables are ideal for growing in backyard gardens. Their soft, feathery green tops look great among the other crops, and they don't take up much space. There are even short, round varieties that grow happily in pots. Carrots have many uses – they are the indispensable vegetable for casseroles, stews, soups and stocks; they are delicious on their own, with chopped parsley, eaten raw, grated in salads, julienned in stir-fries, baked into cakes and are universally admired as a juice vegetable par excellence. You'll never wonder what to do with your bumper crop of carrots.

in the garden

The delicate foliage of carrots is a clue to their fragile constitution. They are frost-tender, so don't plant in autumn where the winters are cold. Nor do they like hot, dry weather. Autumn and early spring are ideal times for sowing in Mediterranean and frost-free temperate gardens.

Like all root crops, carrots like a soft soil mix. Break up all clods and reduce all organic matter to fine particles otherwise they'll be misshapen where the going's too tough.

Add a general garden fertiliser or pelleted poultry manure as the soil is worked over. Drag through a trowel or press on a rake handle to form shallow furrows for the seeds. Carrot seeds are very fine and tend to stick together. They can be mixed with fine sand to distribute them evenly. Otherwise, lightly roughen up the soil in the furrow after the seeds have been dropped in. Seedlings emerge in 2-3 weeks. Sometimes carrots are sown with radish seeds, which are much larger. The radishes germinate sooner, their leaves keep weeds at bay while the carrots are immature, and they are harvested well before they begin to compete with the carrots for root space.

Thin when the seedlings are tiny and again as small carrots start to form. These are the tiny foretastes of the gatherings to come. Leave 5cm (2") between the remaining carrots to allow enough room for their ultimate size. Keep well watered, weed-free and mound up the soil if the carrot tops start to show above the soil. Sunlight turns carrots green. They are still edible, but look less attractive.

Check their size after about 3 months. Pull out a carrot or run your fingers around the top under the soil. If it's the right size, take as many as you need for each occasion, leaving the others in the ground. However, don't leave the stragglers too long as they'll become woody. Sow follow-up plantings each month. Parsnips grow similarly.

preserving the crop

STORING	Store carrots in vegetable storage bags in the refrigerator. Baby carrots will keep for 2-3 days while larger carrots can be kept for about a week.
FREEZING	Carrots can be blanched and frozen whole, if baby, or otherwise sliced (see Freezing, page 113); freeze for up to 10 months. Grated carrot can also be blanched and frozen but doesn't keep as long. It's useful to have on hand to add to casseroles and stir-fries.
PICKLING	Carrots can be pickled. Cook for a very short time only, and pack into hot sterilised jars (see Bottling, page 114); pour over a hot, spiced vinegar mixture and seal while hot. Leave for a couple of weeks before serving with antipasto platters or ploughman's lunches. They will keep for up to 6 months.

for the table

to prepare

• There is no need to peel carrots; they'll lose most of their vitamins if you do. Just wash thoroughly and remove the tops.

• Carrots can be boiled, steamed or microwaved, but remember not to overdo it. They should be crisp rather than limp.

• Children often prefer carrots raw, and when they're just pulled from the garden and washed, they have even more appeal.

to serve

• Cut raw carrots into batons and serve as part of a crudités platter.

• Grated carrots and fresh mint make an interesting and easy salad.

• Grated carrot can be added to potato cakes; serve with a dob of butter.

• Add grated carrot, squeezed out in kitchen paper, to a spicy apple cake. Eat while still warm.

• Start the day with freshly squeezed apple and carrot juice; add pineapple juice for extra zing. Other popular combinations are carrot, orange and beetroot or celery; carrot, orange and ginger; and carrot, ginger and silver beet.

• Roast whole carrots in olive oil and toss with crushed garlic, thyme or rosemary sprigs, and sprinkle with sea salt.

• For an easy carrot dip, cook grated carrot in fresh orange juice over low heat until the liquid has evaporated. When cool, blend with yogurt, then stir in chopped fresh mint, dried currants and grated ginger. Serve with assorted crudités, such as carrot, cucumber and pepper sticks.

• Combine thin strips of carrot with watercress, lamb's lettuce, snow pea sprouts, roasted pecan nuts and segmented orange. Toss with orange juice and olive oil.

• A carrot raita is just the thing to take the edge off a fiery curry; cook fresh curry leaves, dried red chilli and black mustard seeds in vegetable oil until fragrant. Combine with grated carrot and yogurt.

carrot cakes with cream cheese icing

⅓ cup (80ml) vegetable oil

⅓ cup (75g) caster sugar

1 egg

2 medium carrots (240g), grated coarsely

¼ cup (30g) finely chopped walnuts

¾ cup (110g) self-raising flour

¼ teaspoon bicarbonate of soda

½ teaspoon mixed spice

cream cheese icing

20g butter, softened

60g cream cheese, softened

¾ cup (120g) icing sugar

1 Preheat oven to 180°C/160°C. Grease 8 holes of a 12-hole (½-cup/125ml) oval friand pan.

2 Beat oil, sugar and egg in small bowl with electric mixer until thick and pale. Transfer mixture to large bowl; stir in carrot, nuts and sifted dry ingredients. Spoon mixture into pan holes; bake about 20 minutes. Stand cakes in pan 5 minutes before turning, top-side up, onto wire rack to cool.

3 To make cream cheese icing, beat butter and cream cheese in small bowl with electric mixer until light and fluffy. Gradually beat in sifted icing sugar.

4 Spread cold cakes with cream cheese icing. Serve topped with halved walnuts, if you like.

prep + cook time 40 minutes (+ cooling) **makes** 8

orange and maple glazed baby carrots with hazelnuts

30g butter

800g baby carrots, trimmed, peeled

2 teaspoons finely grated orange rind

¼ cup (60ml) orange juice

2 tablespoons dry white wine

2 tablespoons maple syrup

½ cup (70g) coarsely chopped roasted hazelnuts

1 Melt butter in large frying pan; cook carrots, turning occasionally, until almost tender.

2 Add rind, juice, wine and syrup; bring to the boil. Simmer, uncovered, until liquid has almost evaporated and carrots are tender and caramelised.

3 Serve carrots sprinkled with nuts.

prep + **cook time** 25 minutes **serves** 4

dhal and carrot soup

1 tablespoon peanut oil

1 medium brown onion (150g), chopped coarsely

2 cloves garlic, crushed

1 tablespoon ground cumin

1 tablespoon ground coriander

2 teaspoons garam masala

5 medium carrots (600g), chopped coarsely

8 cups (2 litres) vegetable stock

4 cups (1 litre) water

½ cup (100g) brown lentils

½ cup (100g) yellow split peas

½ cup (100g) red lentils

2 tablespoons coarsely chopped fresh coriander

1 Heat oil in large saucepan; cook onion and garlic, stirring, until onion softens. Stir in cumin, ground coriander and garam masala, stirring, until fragrant. Add carrot; cook, stirring, 2 minutes.

2 Add stock and the water to pan; bring to the boil. Add brown lentils and peas; reduce heat, simmer, uncovered, 40 minutes.

3 Add red lentils; simmer, uncovered, 10 minutes or until tender.

4 Blend or process half the soup until smooth; stir into remaining soup in pan. Stir in chopped coriander; serve with a dollop of yogurt and sprinkle with extra chopped fresh coriander, if you like.

prep + **cook time** 1 hour 15 minutes **serves** 8

autumn fruit

Autumn fruits are robust, dependable, earthily fragrant and most often storable. Harvesting new-season fruit is always a delight, but the first bite of a nature-chilled crisp apple, licking the juice of a perfectly ripe pear, and smelling the heady aroma of a sun-warmed fig make the season sing. Twining vines of grapes and kiwifruit drape themselves with golden hues before their leaves drop; these ornamental fruits are able to dress the table purely in their own right.

grapes

in the garden

Grapes grow in most climates found in the UK. They prefer dry air rather than humidity where they often develop mildew-spotted leaves. This problem, however, usually arises after fruiting, so many people have successfully grown grapes even in humid zones with varieties that can cope better in these conditions.

There are many grape varieties: purple or white, seedless or seeded, for eating or for wine. Your local nursery can advise on what grows well in your area.

Grapes grow very easily from cuttings. Plant them in winter and mark the site as it's so easy to mow over the mere sticks or break them as you pass. They will grow easily from cuttings taken from winter prunings.

In early spring, the buds become furred and fat. Once they burst into leaf, the new stems grow at a rapid rate. The tiny bunch-of-grape flowers are sweetly scented. In very dry weather, soak the roots once a week.

The vine is a very generous climber, and can create a sheltered dining area under a pergola in a single season, and will form a dense cover within two seasons.

Birds and bees will want their share, so pick grape bunches regularly and keep the area beneath the vine clear of debris. Handle the bunches gently so you don't remove any bloom, and always cut, rather than break, the stems.

Pruning is essential in late autumn or winter if the vine is to remain productive and shapely. For the home garden, growing it along a strong fence or as a standard will keep it low. Cut back hard to a leaf node on sturdy wood and remove all the cross-connecting stems. When training a grape vine to grow high, such as over a pergola, remove all side shoots until it has reached the desired height and a thick trunk will develop. Treat the spreading top growth as described above.

In cold areas, grapes have to be kept in a greenhouse. The vines are pruned and laid on the ground for filling with sap and speedy growth in spring.

for the table

to serve

• Simply wash and enjoy fresh.

• Add to tossed green salads and, of course, fruit salad.

• Thread grapes onto toothpicks, freeze and serve after a hot and spicy curry.

preserving the crop

STORING	Store table grapes in a vegetable storage bag in the refrigerator for a week or so, bringing them to room temperature before eating.
FREEZING	Grapes can be frozen but must be eaten that way and not defrosted.
PICKLING	Pack grapes into hot sterilised jars (see Bottling, page 114); pour over a hot sugar syrup flavoured with spices and a high proportion of liqueur, then seal while hot and store for a couple of weeks before using. They will keep for about 6 months at room temperature, but once opened must be refrigerated and used quickly. Serve with plain cakes or ice-creams.
BOTTLING	Grapes can also be made into jelly but need the addition of apples or a setting agent. Pour hot jelly into hot sterilised jars (see Bottling, page 114) and seal while hot. Store in a cool dry place for up to a year. Once opened, they must be stored in the refrigerator.

white figs

purple figs

quince

figs

in the garden

The gnarled framework of a fig tree stands starkly bare in winter in all but very mild climates. It will happily grow in a wide range of conditions, though it may need protection where it is very cold.

Select a variety recommended for your area, either green (called white), brown or purple fruited, whatever pleases you most. The darkest fruits make the darkest jam. Little pruning is required, and fertiliser applied in spring and late summer will keep it happy.

Birds will no doubt invade during the fruiting season, so nets over the tree may well be necessary – try to keep the fruit well inside the netting. Fruit ripened on the tree is the sweetest.

for the table

to serve

• Eat fresh.

• Drizzle split fresh figs with maple syrup and cook under a hot grill until warmed through. Serve filled with mascarpone cheese.

• A caramelised spiced fig sauce is the perfect accompaniment to pan-fried pork cutlets, grilled chicken breast fillets and pan-fried white fish fillets.

• Place figs in individual, blind-baked pastry shells; surround figs with a ground almond, sugar and egg mixture. Bake for 20 minutes or until the figs are soft and the mixture is set.

quince

in the garden

The large blossoms of quince in spring are handsomely restrained and the whole tree is attractive throughout the year. The fruit has a furry, golden skin, hard, white flesh and an exquisite aroma. Most quince flesh turns a beautiful rich pink, as if by magic, as it cooks, and all produce a claret-red liquid as they reduce to a jelly. 'Lusitanica' doesn't cook to pink but 'Meech's Prolific', 'Early Prolific', 'Champion' and 'Rea's Mammoth' can be relied upon to do so. 'Vranja' colours well.

Quinces are tolerant of damp soil but don't like very wet roots.

preserving the crop

STORING Store in a cool, dry place for several weeks (if making jelly or jam, don't store for too long as the pectin reduces on storing).

FREEZING Blanched quince wedges can be frozen for up to 3 months (see Freezing, page 113). Best used frozen, not thawed.

PICKLING Jelly or quince paste keeps almost indefinitely in an airtight container. Quinces can also be pickled (see Bottling, page 114).

preserving the crop

STORING	Store figs in a single layer in the refrigerator for 2 days. After this, they start to give off a sticky juice.
FREEZING	Figs are not suitable to freeze.
PICKLING	Preserve their flavour by making jam.
DRYING	Halved figs can be oven-dried (see Drying, page 115). Set the temperature at the lowest setting and leave overnight or until dried. Store in an airtight container in a cool, dry place.

green kiwifruit

yellow kiwifruit

kiwifruit

in the garden

These small, brown furry vine fruits were once known as 'Chinese gooseberries' until farmers in New Zealand discovered they excelled at growing them and bred new, improved varieties. They are now marketed worldwide as kiwifruit and the 'Chinese' name is all but gone. Their almost unbelievable bright green colour, soft flesh and sharp, sweet taste have become standard additions in fruit salads and desserts.

Kiwifruit, with their downy coats, grow on an equally downy, deciduous vine that clambers upwards by twisting its strong stems around trellises, pergolas, verandah rails or through trees. A kiwifruit vine can be a useful alternative to grapes as a summer sun shield and will allow winter sun through as the leaves drop.

For the best growth, kiwifruit need a long warm summer and a cool, frost-free winter. Their roots are shallow and fibrous, so keep them well watered throughout summer.

Spread a thick mulch of old manure, well-rotted compost or leaf mulch and the complete garden fertiliser of your choice each spring to protect the roots from drying out.

There are male and female plants so you must plant a pair for the spring blossoms to pollinate. If you want to plant more than a pair for extra fruit, one male plant can cope with five females.

The large, rough leaves shield the developing fruit from the sun during summer. In autumn as the leaves fall, the low sun sweetens the fruit. Pick them as you need them before they drop off the vine.

for the table

to serve

• Kiwifruit are high in vitamin C and are very convenient to serve; you only have to peel them. They can also be spooned out like boiled eggs.

• Kiwifruit are best enjoyed as they are. They do not cook well, but can have a flavoured syrup poured over them if you wish for something a little more exotic. Try an orange or mandarin-flavoured liqueur in the syrup.

• Kiwifruit is high in enzymes and can be used as a meat tenderiser. Puree several kiwifruit, add pepper and use as a marinade for meat. Leave for several hours, then discard the marinade and cook the meat as desired.

• Peel kiwifruit and cut into wedges. Combine with passionfruit pulp and some orange-flavoured liqueur for an almost instant sauce.

preserving the crop

STORING	Kiwifruit stores well at room temperature for up to a week. Store separately as the ethylene from other fruit (such as apples and bananas) ripens kiwifruit before you need them. Once they give a little when pressed gently, store in the refrigerator for several days. Like melons, they are best served cool but not too cold.
FREEZING	Kiwifruit are not suitable to freeze.
PICKLING	Jam and chutney can be made from kiwifruit. They must be peeled before use. Spoon the hot jam or chutney into hot sterilised jars (see Bottling, page 114), and seal while still hot. Store for several months.

autumn herbs

The full range of spring and summer herbs is generally available through autumn, but here we pay particular attention to those herbs seemingly designed for the dishes we associate with cooler weather. Rosemary teams up with roasted meats and barbecues, while lemon grass and chilli, essential ingredients in Asian curries and soups, add heat and piquancy. All three are easy to grow in the garden or pots.

in the garden

rosemary

Rosemary is a tough shrub with thin, stiff, aromatic leaves or needles. Its basic form is stoutly upright and dense with pale mauve flowers at the stem tips during autumn and winter. Another variety is prostrate and drapes itself down walls or rocks, or spreads like a mat over the ground. Its flowers are sky-blue.

This plant likes a challenge: seaside sites, strong winds, dry rocky slopes, heavy snow or baking sun, and almost any type of soil, however, it won't survive soggy conditions and doesn't care for shade.

It is the ideal plant for pots and can be formal enough to look and smell impressive on a sunny doorstep or stand shoulder to shoulder with a line-up of potted herbs along a pathway.

When the plant is still small, snip a few leaves at a time until it starts to expand. It does take its time. Rosemary lasts many years, seeing out successions of basil, chervil and parsley, and eventually becomes a sizeable shrub that will need repotting.

lemon grass

Lemon grass is exactly that: a grass. It's perennial and forms a dramatic dense clump of tall, weeping foliage. It also makes a great tufted display in a large pot. Like other grasses, it is hardy as well. Try not to plant it too close to paths or steps as the leaves are sharp to brush against, although its scent is delightfully aromatic.

It grows best in full sun or just dappled shade in well-drained soil, and tolerates most temperate climates. It even tolerates a windy site.

Give it a good soak around the roots every week in dry weather and, provided you don't use every cane that develops, in time it will form a large clump.

The leaves can be used fresh or dried as a tea but they will become ragged and rust-spotted during winter. You can either ignore its looks or, in early spring, cut it back to 15cm (6") above the ground, thus leaving the stems to use while new leaves push through the centre and unfurl.

The fresh stalks and leaves have a clean lemon-like aroma due to its high citral content, the same essential oil that is also present in lemon peel.

preserving the crop

STORING ROSEMARY	Store fresh stalks in a plastic bag in the refrigerator.
FREEZING ROSEMARY	Rosemary can be frozen for up to 6 months (see Freezing, page 113). There's no need to chop; freeze the stalks on a flat tray and, when frozen, transfer them to a plastic freezer bag; the needles will break off from the stems.
DRYING ROSEMARY	Fresh is best, but home-dried rosemary (see Drying, page 115) keeps its flavour longer than commercially dried rosemary.
STORING LEMON GRASS	The fresher the better, so leave in the garden as long as you can. If you must store fresh lemon grass, cut as little as possible from the stalks, leaving the root end intact, wrap in damp paper towel in a plastic bag, and store in the refrigerator for a couple of days only.
FREEZING LEMON GRASS	Can be chopped and frozen in small batches (see Freezing, page 113). It will keep in the freezer for up to 6 months.
DRYING LEMON GRASS	Dried lemon grass is integral to some Asian dishes but don't keep for longer than a couple of months or you will be disappointed in the taste (see Drying, page 115).
STORING CHILLIES	Chillies should be stored in a cool, dry place for up to a week. Pack loosely so air can circulate through them.
FREEZING CHILLIES	Chopped fresh chillies can be frozen for about 6 months. Add them frozen to cooked dishes.
DRYING CHILLIES	Thread chillies onto a thread or string, and hang in an airy place to dry (see Drying, page 115). The heat intensifies on drying, so use with caution.

chillies

Chillies are related to peppers and grow under the same conditions – they demand a frost-free, well-drained, well-watered, sunny site with deeply dug soil that has been well supplied with a complete fertiliser. They don't like alkaline soil so they also like the addition of lime to lower the soil's acidity. Start seedlings indoors if you live where late frosts threaten. Most develop into spreading sub-shrubs 1m (3') or more tall and wide in a season. Chillies flower in spring and summer and the chillies hang on the plants well into winter in mild gardens. Frosts and very cold winds will destroy them. You may be able to prune them down to 15cm (6") in autumn, and in cool and cold zones protect with straw or compost and manure over winter. They will sprout again as the warm weather commences.

Seeds and seedlings are available from nurseries and dried seeds from varieties you have tried are often successful. The heat of chillies is generally rated 1 (mild) to 10 (hottest). Paprika is mild, jalapeño is medium, Thai or birdseye is hot, and the declared winner at 10 is habanero.

Wear disposable gloves when preparing chillies and scrub the chopping board well. Always wash your hands after handling chillies.

for the table

to serve

• Rosemary sprigs added to a bottle of red wine vinegar along with a few peppercorns makes a beautiful salad dressing.

• For a smoky rosemary taste, add sprigs to the fire when barbecuing lamb.

• When making sweet chilli dipping sauce for fresh spring rolls, delete some of the chilli and add chopped fresh lemon grass instead.

• Use lemon grass as giant skewers for chicken and pork. Quarter the stalks before threading meat cubes onto them; cook on a ridged grill pan or barbecue.

• For chilli-flavoured oil, heat 12 small fresh chillies in peanut oil until warm but not hot. Remove from heat and steep at room temperature for 2 hours. Drain the oil into hot, sterilised bottles and seal while hot. Store at room temperature for 6 months.

stir-fried tofu with vegetables and lemon grass

2 teaspoons sesame oil
400g firm tofu, diced into 1cm pieces
1 large red pepper (350g), sliced thinly
750g baby pak choi, chopped coarsely
2 x 10cm sticks fresh lemon grass (40g), chopped finely
2 cloves garlic, crushed
½ cup loosely packed fresh coriander leaves

1 Heat oil in wok; stir-fry tofu, pepper, pak choi, lemon grass and garlic until vegetables are just tender. Stir in coriander.

2 Serve stir-fry with lemon wedges, if desired.

prep + **cook time** 15 minutes **serves** 4

note Lemon grass is a tall, thick, tropical grass with leaves at the top and a solid whitish portion, several inches long, at the base of the stem. When using fresh lemon grass, use only the white lower portion of the stem. (In Asia, the leaves are often used to make a lemon tea.) Peel away the tough outer layers to reveal the pale lower section of the stem; use a sharp knife to trim the base. If using in soups, syrups or casseroles, press the stem with the flat side of a large knife to bruise and release the flavour. If using in stir-fries, cut the pale section thinly across the fibres.

rosemary lamb skewers

8 sprigs fresh rosemary

600g lamb mince

1 egg yolk

⅓ cup (25g) stale breadcrumbs

2 cloves garlic, crushed

1 tablespoon tomato paste

¼ cup (60ml) olive oil

1 large brown onion (200g), sliced thinly

1 tablespoon plain flour

1 cup (250ml) beef stock

2 medium tomatoes (300g), chopped coarsely

1 Remove two-thirds of the leaves from the bottom part of each rosemary sprig to make skewers. Finely chop 2 teaspoons of the leaves and reserve.

2 Combine mince, egg yolk, breadcrumbs, garlic, paste and reserved rosemary in medium bowl. Shape lamb mixture into sausage shapes on skewers.

3 Heat 1 tablespoon of the oil in large frying pan; cook skewers until browned and cooked through. Remove from pan.

4 Heat remaining oil in same pan; cook onion until soft. Add flour; cook, stirring, until mixture bubbles and thickens. Gradually stir in stock until smooth. Add tomato; cook until gravy boils and thickens.

5 Serve rosemary lamb skewers with gravy.

prep + cook time 35 minutes **serves** 4

chilli coriander jam

8 large tomatoes (2kg), cored

⅓ cup (80ml) olive oil

10 cloves garlic, peeled

4cm piece fresh ginger (20g), grated

10 fresh small red Thai chillies, stems removed

2 tablespoons cumin seeds

2 tablespoons black mustard seeds

¾ cup (180ml) red wine vinegar

¼ cup (60ml) fish sauce

1¼ cups (335g) grated palm sugar

1 tablespoon ground turmeric

½ cup finely chopped fresh coriander leaves and roots

1 Preheat fan oven to 180°C/160°C.

2 Rub tomatoes with oil, place in roasting pan; roast about 30 minutes or until soft but not coloured.

3 Blend or process garlic, ginger, chillies and seeds until chopped and well combined. Transfer mixture to large heavy-based pan; add tomatoes, vinegar, sauce, sugar and turmeric. Simmer about 2 hours or until thick and jammy.

4 Blend mixture, in batches, until chopped coarsely; stir in coriander. Spoon into hot sterilised jars; seal while still hot.

prep + cook time 2 hours 45 minutes

makes about 6 cups

note Store in a cool dry place for up to 6 months. Refrigerate jam once opened.

the winter garden

There are two schools of thought on winter. There are those people who dread it, hide away and grizzle about the cold air, the clothing layers, the dampness that seems to cling to everything and the cost of heating. Then there are those who relish the battle that nature thrusts their way, the extra energy and 'go' that cool air engenders, the brilliance of sunlit days or the haze of cloudy ones, and long cook-ups in the kitchen.

Across most of the country there'll be scurries out to harvest winter vegetables, and a prowl around to view the cold and wind-wracked berries and skeletonised flower tops, and to look for early signs of spring. Indoors, there will be growers' lists and seed catalogues to peruse, and some early seedling trays to establish to get things started.

Underneath the cold, hard sometimes frozen ground, the soil cries out for digging and revitalising in preparation for the series of replacement crops that warm conditions will allow.

The frosty, cold, damp, wet season will be flattening all in its path, and the longed-for rain will be soaking through the soil layers. The sound of roots, stems and leaves refilling is almost audible and plants start to stand up proud again until a polar blast makes them reconsider. In protected sites where the ground is dry and workable, there are maintenance tasks to match.

In contrast, in subtropical areas, gardeners need to be wary of drying winds. The sun is not as hot as in summer, but if the signs are ignored, plants will die. There'll be supplies of winter vegetables and herbs, and little insect damage.

In winter, gardeners everywhere busy themselves with what they consider to be the season's appropriate business.

Winter is a great help to gardeners – especially if you garden on a heavy soil. The repeated action of freezing and thawing that occurs naturally in winter is exactly what heavy soils need to break them up. Called 'weathering', it helps you to see the benefits of heavy, repeated frost action. Plus winter is great for killing all of last season's pests!

So let's view the winter garden bounty.

sow now	harvest now
sow aubergine, broad beans, carrots, cauliflower, celeriac, cucumber, lettuce (with protection), onions, Asian greens, parsley, peppers (with protection), rocket, tomatoes (with protection).	in the vegetable garden chard, chicory, Jerusalem artichokes, kale, leeks, winter lettuce, spinach.
plant asparagus, garlic, rhubarb, shallots.	in the herb garden bay, rosemary, sage.

the brassicas

The brassicas, better known as the cabbage group of vegetables, are the stalwarts of winter. Rounded, florid and bulbous with wonderful foliage colours from silver, grey-green, yellow to bright green, these over-sized vegetables make striking crops when the winter garden beds might otherwise be bare.

Brassicas actually prefer the cold conditions of winter and are not much pleased by hot temperatures and the baking sun. They make ideal home crops during that time of the year when the garden has withdrawn for winter and gardeners themselves prefer the great indoors.

The brassica family is a large one and includes cabbages, cauliflower, broccoli, Brussels sprouts and kale. These are the slow-growing members of the tribe that can take anywhere between 3-5 months to be ready to pick.

Also part of the brassica family are the quick-growing Asian greens that have had such a culinary impact in the West over recent years. Pak choi (Chinese chard), Chinese flat cabbage (tatsoi) and Chinese flowering cabbage (choy sum) are ready to harvest in 6-8 weeks. The salad feathers of mizuna are the speed champions with early leaves harvestable in just 20 days.

Over the following pages we feature the most common brassicas grown in home gardens. The fast-growing Asian greens are ideal for staggered planting and harvesting to ensure a steady supply for quick stir-fries and winter salads. The slow-growing brassicas are tantalising to watch as they solidly progress, their majestic leaves unfurl and their large, tightly-packed hearts and flower buds form.

general cultivation

Like all leafy crops, brassicas do best in soil that has been well-manured a month prior to planting to make it light and full of organic matter. Two weeks before planting, add a generous supply of nitrogen-rich fertiliser and a sprinkling of lime so all their required trace elements will be available from the soil.

If you haven't room to spare for a month of growing nothing, brassicas can be planted as a follow-on to beans; they'll make use of the nitrogen stored in the bean roots. However, seedlings will still need extra fertiliser and lime to boost them along.

The fast-growing brassicas are usually planted from seed in-situ or in seed trays, and can be harvested and thinned as they develop.

The slow-growers are usually raised in seedling trays or shallow pots, or bought as seedlings and planted out when the soil is ready. This gives them a head start and allows their roots to become established.

If wanting to raise crops from seed, cover the seeds with 0.5cm (¼") of sand or seed-raising mixture. They'll emerge in 6-10 days with two almost heart-shaped leaves. Once they've developed their miniature, true leaves, thin them in the garden or plant out seedlings 50-75cm (20-30") apart for slow-growers or 10-15cm (4-6") for speedsters. Firm them in well.

Brassicas must be planted in full sun with well-drained soil to reduce the risk of fungal problems. It's a good idea to raise the soil into mounds or furrows and plant the seedlings on the top. Always keep well watered. Irrigation by means of the furrows is preferable to overhead waterings.

preserving the crop (broccoli)

STORING	Store in a vegetable storage bag in the refrigerator for up to 3 days. It's also possible to store broccoli, with stems in a container of water, covered by a vegetable storage bag, for about 5 days.
FREEZING	Broccoli can be blanched and frozen for several months. Pack into rigid containers (see Freezing, page 113). Cook when needed in boiling water, unthawed. Cooked and pureed broccoli freezes very well for several months.

green cauliflower

broccoli

pests and diseases

The whole brassica family is the mainstay in the life cycle of the cabbage moth and the cabbage white butterfly, both of which deposit their eggs on the leaves. The leaves are then consumed by the developing caterpillars. The leaf surfaces are eaten first, then whole sections of leaf. The cabbage moth caterpillar will even eat right into the heart of the cabbage.

Pick the caterpillars off by hand as soon as you see them or spray with an insecticide.

Aphids can gather among the grey foliage, and weaken the plant as they suck out its nourishment. Keep alert for mass attacks and pick off, hose off or spray.

broccoli

What can be more fetching to a gardening cook than a bouquet of broccoli? And that's exactly what a head of broccoli is: a cluster of buds harvested from the centre of rich blue-green leaves.

in the garden

For general soil preparation and cultivation notes, see page 86.

Broccoli grows best from spring sowings outdoors, and will develop strongly and be more resistant to insect attack if given liquid fertiliser every 2-3 weeks.

Its bouquet of tight buds at the top of the stem is produced in 3-4 months. Always cut broccoli early when the buds are still tightly furled and coloured either purplish or green depending on the variety. If left too long before harvesting, the buds start to open and the flavour and texture change, and stems with yellow flowers form.

After the initial harvest, the plants start to produce small stem offshoots of broccoli for another month or two. These small shoots are harvestable and good to eat. However, if any of the florets are allowed to ripen to yellow and open, the plant is satisfied it has run its course and will start to fade. So, for the longest possible harvest, trim the side shoots until they become too small.

Some broccoli varieties have been specially bred to grow during warm weather so plant these for an early autumn crop.

'Romanesco' is a recently developed variety with lime-green flower-heads and tightly spiralled cones. It is sweetly flavoured and dramatic to serve whole, but it behaves more like cauliflower in that it does not produce successive shoots.

for the table

to prepare

• Aphids, bugs and caterpillars love to hide in the florets of broccoli, so soak for a short time in cold water and shake gently to release unwanted dinner guests.

• Broccoli can be boiled, steamed, stir-fried or microwaved. Cut the florets from the stalk and use separately. Covering broccoli while cooking will preserve a stronger flavour.

• The stems are edible, but need to have their tough outer skin removed before using raw in salads or tossing in a stir-fry (avoid over-cooking).

• Try saving the stems and cook all at once in an Asian-style oyster sauce.

baby broccoli

cauliflower

Chinese cabbage

to serve

• Use broccoli florets to carry strong flavours such as garlic and lemon. Use only lemon rind as the acid from the juice darkens and wrinkles the broccoli stems.

• Dotted with anchovy butter, steamed broccoli becomes a great accompaniment to a simple meal.

• Toss broccoli florets with brown butter and toasted almonds.

• Add finely chopped broccoli to a pasta sauce with Italian sausage and lots of garlic.

• Broccoli makes great soup. Cook in chicken stock with fresh herbs and garlic; puree and add a dash of cream for a very elegant starter.

cauliflower

Here's another flower-bud head that is prized when it's densely packed and its 'curds' (just like fresh cheese) are pure in colour and firm. Straight from the garden, the cauliflower will break apart with a snap. Cauliflower is always less odorous when cooked fresh.

in the garden

For general soil preparation and cultivation notes, see page 86.

Cauliflowers are the fussiest of the brassicas to grow. They are very sensitive to soil pH. Diseases (such as club root) and deformed growth are caused by soil that is too acidic. Always add a generous handful of garden lime to each square metre (square yard) of soil when preparing the garden beds 2 weeks before planting. Sprinkle another dusting of lime over the soil 1 week after the seedlings have been planted.

Cauliflowers are generally ready to harvest in 4-6 months and need cool temperatures and full sun to grow well. Start to raise seeds in mid- and late spring so you can plant them before midsummer. Seedlings are also available from nurseries. Plant seedlings out firmly (so that you can tug the leaf and rip it) 60-80cm (24-32") apart.

The young cauliflower plants need to be well established by the time winter begins as the cool weather is essential for the cauliflower heads to develop. In the heat of summer the heads start to open and break up.

As the heads form, protect them from the sun by tying their large leaves into a teepee above or breaking them and folding over the white heads. The heads will yellow if exposed to the sun. The leaves of some varieties grow around the head and automatically shelter it. Peep regularly under their covers to watch for when the flowers become tight and solid. Harvest them straight away or they'll open out.

Unlike broccoli, cauliflowers put their all into one flower, so there is no repeat harvest. It is a good idea when planting the seedlings to hold a few back and plant 2-3 weeks later to stagger the crop.

Several white cauliflower varieties are available and differ only in the length of time they take to form. 'Alverda' is a variety with greenish curds. Pink, green, purple and even orange varieties are available. Their flavours are as individual as their colourings.

Mini cauliflowers are formed by planting seedlings only 25-30cm (10-12") apart and harvesting the small heads as soon as they reach 10cm (4") across, in about 4 months. Keep up follow-on plantings as the cauliflowers are harvested one by one.

for the table

to prepare

• Soak the florets in cold water for a short period before cooking to flush out any bugs or caterpillars.

• Cauliflower can be boiled, steamed, stir-fried or microwaved.

savoy cabbage

green cabbage

red cabbage

to serve

• For a delicious soup, cook cauliflower in a strong chicken stock with onions; blend, adding some fresh dill sprigs. Return to heat and warm through, adding enough cream to make a thick, but smooth, soup.

• Steam cauliflower and top with crisped chopped bacon, toasted breadcrumbs and a drizzle of butter; brown under a hot grill.

• Add cauliflower to a salad of red and yellow pepper, tomatoes and strips of crisped salami. Toss with an Italian dressing.

• Cauliflower cheese is an age-old favourite. Any leftovers can be blended until smooth and thinned with a little milk to make an instant soup.

preserving the crop

STORING Cover the cauliflower with paper towel before storing in a vegetable storage bag in the refrigerator for up to a week.

FREEZING Cauliflower can be blanched and frozen (see Freezing, page 113) for up to 4 months. Store in rigid containers so the florets do not break up.

cabbage and Brussels sprouts

Cabbages and Brussels sprouts are both stout winter growers. For general soil preparation and cultivation notes, see page 86.

cabbage

Of all the brassicas, cabbages are the most tolerant of warm conditions. There are varieties that can be planted to provide a continuous harvest right through the year in most climates. Cabbages can be picked small or left to become full-sized, but their holding ability is better in cooler weather. They start to crack open, even rot, if left too long.

Sow spring cabbages in summer, sow summer cabbages in spring and sow winter cabbages in spring to harvest around 20-36 weeks later.

There are an astounding number of varieties. There are those with conical heads such as 'Sugarloaf' or 'Durham Early', which are quick maturing for speedy crops. Others develop tight, round heads and varieties include the fast-growing minis and 'Earliball' and the larger, slower winter regulars like 'January King' (for the winter) and 'Primo'.

Colours vary from deep to light green, grey, purple-green and rich beet red. Leaf textures offer more variety with some tightly stretched and smooth around the head and others rumpled and creased, like the 'Savoy' cabbage.

Then there are the kales, which are loose-leaf cabbages. The leaves fan out in the same manner as silver beet and spinach. Their young leaves, and also the older leaves, though strongly flavoured, can be cooked, and they are particularly suited to stir-frying. There are plain-leafed varieties that can stand nearly 1m (3') tall like 'cottages' and 'chou moellier'. Others are curly and fringed like the 'Scotch', 'Tall Green Curled' and 'Ornamental'. 'Palm Tree Kale', or Italian cabbage, has dark grey, crumpled leaves.

Experiment with cabbage varieties that you have never tried before. Certainly choose according to culinary desires, but also be adventurous and use cabbages as ornamental winter garden features for there are few vegetables as showy and dramatic. You'll be rewarded with a wintertime chorus of cabbage leaf shapes and colours, all with a sweet cabbage flavour.

kale

Brussels sprouts

Brussels sprouts

Fortunately Britain is blessed with exactly the right long cold winter that favours Brussels sprouts. They grow in the same manner as their brassica relatives but develop a tall, strong stem. Feed regularly with liquid fertiliser and mound up the soil around the stem base to support it. The more leaves that develop up the stem, the more sprouts you'll be able to gather from the leaf junctions.

As the sprouts start to form near the base, strip the lower leaves from the stem with a sideways pull so the sprouts can develop round and firm. You'll be able to harvest in 4-7 months.

Gather the sprouts as they develop, or cut the stem at the growing point when it's about 40cm (16") tall and they'll all mature at once. Discard those sprouts that start to burst open; the ideal sprout is tightly furled and about 5cm (2") in diameter.

As soon as the buds start to form, remember to spread around a slug and snail deterrent as both of them relish such new morsels.

preserving the crop

STORING Cabbages are best stored whole in the refrigerator. Once cut, use within a few days.

Brussels sprouts can be stored in a vegetable storage bag for several days in the refrigerator.

FREEZING Shred cabbage, blanch, then freeze for up to 6 months (see Freezing, page 113). Cook from frozen.

Brussels sprouts can be blanched and frozen for up to 6 months in rigid containers to keep their shape.

PICKLING Pickled red cabbage is popular. Salt the cabbage and stand overnight; rinse well the following day. Pack the cabbage into hot sterilised jars (see Bottling, page 114). Heat white vinegar with sugar and spices, such as cloves and cinnamon, until boiling and pour over cabbage in jars; seal while hot.

for the table

to prepare

• Cabbage and Brussels sprouts can be boiled, steamed, microwaved or eaten raw. Avoid adding large amounts of water. Rinse cabbage, shake off excess water and cook, covered. Don't overcook as the smell and taste becomes unpalatable.

to serve

• Sprinkle cabbage generously with crisp chopped pancetta, garlic and a little butter.

• Finely shred cabbage and add to a pan of boiling water with a spoonful of caraway seeds; return to the boil, then drain and add a knob of butter before serving.

• Stir-fry shredded cabbage until crisp; drizzle with sesame oil and sprinkle with sesame seeds.

• For a mixed cabbage coleslaw, whisk some oil, cider vinegar and Dijon mustard together in a large bowl. Toss through some finely shredded green cabbage, red cabbage and Chinese cabbage, a coarsely grated carrot and some thinly sliced green onion.

• Lightly steam Brussels sprouts, then toss in a hot pan with olive oil and fresh chestnuts; serve with grilled steak.

• Toss halved Brussels sprouts in melted butter. Add some white wine, chicken stock and a handful of sultanas. Cook, covered, until sprouts are soft, remove lid and cook until liquid is almost absorbed. Serve with grilled or roasted meats.

piccalilli

1 tablespoon salt

1kg vegetables, coarsely chopped (see notes)

4 cups (1 litre) white vinegar

1 cup (220g) white sugar

1 tablespoon ground turmeric

1 tablespoon mustard powder

3 cloves garlic, sliced

4 fresh small red Thai chillies, halved lengthways

⅓ cup (75g) cornflour

1 Sprinkle salt over vegetables; stand overnight. Rinse under cold water; drain well.

2 Combine vinegar, sugar, turmeric, mustard powder, garlic and chilli in large pan. Bring to the boil, add vegetables; simmer, covered, about 5 minutes or until vegetables are just tender.

3 Take ½ cup of liquid from pan and blend with cornflour; stir into pan. Return to the boil; boil about 3 minutes or until thickened. Pour into hot sterilised jars and seal while hot (see notes).

4 Store in a cool, dry place for 4 weeks before using. Once opened, store in the refrigerator.

prep + **cook time** 25 minutes (+ standing) **makes** about 8 cups

notes Use a mixture of cauliflower, carrots, celery, green tomatoes, cucumber and pickling onions. Drain away some of the liquid before bottling, if the mixture seems too wet.

Brussels sprouts with cream and almonds

50g butter

⅓ cup (25g) flaked almonds

1kg Brussels sprouts, trimmed, halved

2 cloves garlic, crushed

300ml cream

1 Melt 10g of the butter in large frying pan; cook nuts, stirring, until browned lightly, remove from pan.

2 Melt remaining butter in same pan; cook sprouts and garlic, stirring, until sprouts are browned lightly. Add cream; bring to the boil. Simmer, uncovered, until sprouts are tender and sauce thickens slightly.

3 Serve sprout mixture sprinkled with nuts.

prep + **cook time** 10 minutes **serves** 4

cauliflower gratin

1 small cauliflower (750g), trimmed,
  broken into large florets

50g butter

¼ cup (35g) plain flour

1½ cups (375ml) hot milk

½ cup (60g) coarsely grated cheddar cheese

¼ cup (20g) finely grated Parmesan cheese

1 tablespoon packaged breadcrumbs

1 Preheat fan oven to 220°C/200°C.

2 Boil, steam or microwave cauliflower until tender;
drain. Place in medium shallow ovenproof dish.

3 Meanwhile, melt butter in medium pan, add flour;
cook, stirring, until mixture bubbles and thickens.
Gradually stir in milk until smooth; cook, stirring,
until mixture boils and thickens. Remove from heat,
stir in cheeses.

4 Pour cheese sauce over cauliflower; sprinkle
with breadcrumbs. Bake, in oven, about 15 minutes
or until browned lightly.

prep + cook time 30 minutes **serves** 6

note If you can find them, use six baby cauliflowers,
(weighing a total of 750g), instead. There is no
need to break them into florets, just microwave
then bake them whole.

crêpes with creamy broccoli

8 frozen French-style crêpes (400g), thawed

¼ cup (20g) grated Parmesan cheese

broccoli filling

750g broccoli, trimmed, chopped coarsely

30g butter

2 green onions, chopped coarsely

1 tablespoon wholemeal plain flour

½ cup (125ml) milk

½ cup (125ml) cream

pinch ground nutmeg

1 Preheat fan oven to 180°C/160°C.

2 Make broccoli filling. Divide filling between
crêpes; fold crêpes into triangles.

3 Place crêpes in oiled ovenproof dish; sprinkle with
cheese. Bake crêpes, in oven, about 10 minutes or
until cheese has melted and crêpes and filling are
heated through.

broccoli filling Boil, steam or microwave broccoli
until tender; drain. Heat butter in medium pan; cook
onion, stirring, over medium heat, 1 minute. Stir in
flour; cook, stirring, 1 minute. Remove from heat;
gradually stir in combined milk, cream and nutmeg;
stir over high heat until mixture boils and thickens.
Stir in broccoli.

prep + cook time 25 minutes **serves** 4

Asian greens

Asian greens are the speedsters of the brassica family. They all grow very quickly and are best cooked rapidly to preserve their bright green colouring, as it's their stems and leaves that we relish. They are the soft and juicy members of the brassica troupe, and many have a deliciously sharp flavour.

in the garden

Asian greens grow fast and succulent only if hurried along. Start with rich soil and add weekly applications of liquid fertiliser so that their stems and leaves don't become stringy. Frequent water keeps them bulky. Flood the root zone every 3-4 days if the weather is dry, and test the soil with your finger after rain to make sure moisture has soaked through to the roots (often the large leaves deflect light rain showers). Asian greens will not tolerate frosts, but will grow year-round in frost-free areas.

In very small gardens, grow varieties you can harvest leaf by leaf, and plant replacement crops every 2 weeks or so. Move the brassica site every 6 months to deter insects, prevent the build-up of soil diseases and to rest the soil.

A shallow, 30-40cm (12-16") pot filled with very rich potting mix will support a selection of strongly flavoured greens and lettuce for a garden salad mix. It must be in full sun and well watered. Your 'salad bowl' will last a month or two, and so plant a second pot 3-4 weeks after the original to extend supply throughout the season.

Chinese broccoli (gai lan) has long, slender stems, large leaves and a small bud or white flower cluster. When the buds are closed, they are edible but should be removed if open. They can be picked in 8-10 weeks.

Pak choi (bok choy, Chinese chard, baby pak choi) has heavy white stems the same length as its leaves. It takes 5-6 weeks to grow but the odd leaf can be used while it's developing.

Mustard cabbage (gai choy) is more leaf than stem and is ready in 6-8 weeks, odd leaves being available as they grow. When full size, cut off at the roots and cook whole

Chinese flat cabbage (tatsoi, rosette pak choi, komatsuma) forms an open cluster of deep green leaves with brilliant white stems. It spreads out to 30cm (12") like a glorious green posy. Use leaf by leaf or cut off whole. It has a slightly strong flavour and is ready to harvest in 8 weeks.

Chinese flowering cabbage (choy sum) is very similar to Chinese broccoli with long stems, rounded leaves and a small bud or yellow flower cluster. Again, the closed buds are edible while the open buds are not. They can be picked in 8-10 weeks.

Chinese cabbage (wombok) is a tall, elongated cabbage, lighter and less tightly packed, and develops its fully enwrapped form in 8-10 weeks.

Mizuna, another of the brassicas, is described on page 50.

pests and diseases

Asian greens are prone to the same cabbage moth and butterfly caterpillar attacks as the slow-growing brassicas,

preserving the crop

STORING	Store all Asian greens in vegetable storage bags in the refrigerator for 1-2 days only. Chinese cabbage (wombok) will last for longer if stored whole. Once cut though, use as quickly as possible.
FREEZING	These vegetables don't survive the freezing process well.

but their faster growth makes damage less likely. Slugs and snails love the lush, new growth, so protect seedlings as they emerge and keep renewing the baits as the plants develop. Pick slugs off at night by torch light as they feed.

for the table

to prepare

• Harvest all Asian greens as close to preparation as possible. Pick whole, or pick only as much as you need. Only wash when ready to prepare.

• Harvest Chinese flowering cabbage and Chinese broccoli as the flowers open with furled buds.

to serve

• Chinese flowering cabbage can be lightly boiled, steamed or microwaved and served with any butter sauce, although it's traditionally served with oyster sauce or Hollandaise.

• For a quick Chinese flowering cabbage stir-fry, stir-fry some chilli, garlic and ginger for a minute in a hot oiled wok. Add some Chinese flowering cabbage, trimmed into 5cm lengths, and stir-fry until tender. Add some fish sauce and lime juice and stir-fry until hot. Sprinkle with cashews.

• Pak choi and baby pak choi can be boiled, steamed, stir-fried or microwaved. Stir through pancetta, Parmesan and garlic.

• Stir-fry pak choi with garlic and serve with sesame oil and a sprinkling of sesame seeds.

• Chinese cabbage can be used in the same way as green cabbage and is great raw in salads.

• Stuff Chinese cabbage leaves with a pork mince and rice vermicelli filling and steam; drizzle with soy sauce mixed with rice wine just before serving hot.

• For a quick and simple side dish, heat some oil in a wok, add a sliced onion and cook until soft. Add about 2 cups of shredded Chinese cabbage; stir-fry until just wilted, then stir through some soy sauce.

• Chinese flat cabbage can be used in the same way as pak choi or Chinese cabbage. Add raw to salads but remember it has a stronger flavour than pak choi.

• Chinese broccoli needs the tough outer stem layer removed before cooking. Cook the stems first and add the chopped leaves at the end. Great with a little butter, salt and pepper. It's also good stir-fried with pork or chicken.

• Pak choy can be added whole to soups. It is also good served with rich meats such as duck and pork.

• Preserved mustard cabbage can be bought in Asian supermarkets and should be rinsed before using.

• Deep-fry mustard cabbage leaves until translucent and use as a bed for fish and seafood.

• Segment a ruby red grapefruit over a large bowl; add some oil, mustard, mizuna, cashew nuts, red onion and thickly sliced smoked salmon. Toss to combine salad.

mizuna

Chinese broccoli

Chinese flowering cabbage

baby pak choi

steamed Chinese broccoli in oyster sauce

1kg Chinese broccoli, halved
1 tablespoon peanut oil
2 tablespoons oyster sauce
1 tablespoon light soy sauce

1 Boil, steam or microwave Chinese broccoli until tender; drain.

2 Heat oil in wok, add Chinese broccoli and sauces; stir-fry about 2 minutes or until mixture is heated through.

prep + cook time 10 minutes

serves 6 (as an accompaniment)

note Light soy sauce is the best type of soy sauce to use in dishes where the natural colour of the ingredients is to be maintained, such as stir-frying, braising, seasoning soups and for dressing salads. It is fairly thin in consistency and, while paler than the others, it is the saltiest tasting; do not confuse with salt-reduced or low-sodium soy sauces.

pak choi steamed with chilli oil

4 baby pak choi (600g)
1 tablespoon peanut oil
2 cloves garlic, crushed
2 tablespoons light soy sauce
1½ teaspoons hot chilli sauce
2 green onions, sliced
¼ cup fresh coriander leaves
1 fresh small red Thai chilli, sliced thinly

1 Halve pak choi lengthways; place, cut-side up, in large bamboo steamer, drizzle with combined oil, garlic and sauces.

2 Steam pak choi, covered, over large saucepan of simmering water about 5 minutes or until just tender. Serve sprinkled with onion, coriander and chilli.

prep + cook time 10 minutes **serves** 4

spinach & silver beet

These two leafy greens are often confused. Silver beet (or swiss chard) is related to beetroot. It grows in a clump and its leaves are a thing of beauty: tall white stems – or if a rainbow form then yellow, orange, red or pink – with deep green, crinkly leaves that grow to 30-40cm (12-16"). Spinach, on the other hand, stands not quite so tall, has thin stems with clear, green leaves and a delicate, subtle taste.

in the garden

Both spinach and silver beet require well-prepared soil. Dig in plenty of chicken manure and well-matured compost, with a dressing of nitrogen-rich fertiliser 2-3 weeks before planting in a sunny or lightly shaded spot with morning sun. Silver beet prefers full sun. It performs best in the garden as it develops a large root system; if grown in pots, silver beet needs replacing often.

silver beet

Silver beet seeds benefit from a soak in cold water for a few hours. Push the softened seeds down to the first finger joint, spacing them 30-40cm (12-16") apart. Stems and leaves will appear in 2 weeks. They may need thinning as several can emerge from each seed. Mulch and keep well watered. Give liquid feeds every 2 weeks in the cool of the day as fertiliser can burn in sunlight.

Harvest silver beet leaves by breaking off outside leaves with a downward and sideways pull. Always keep 4-5 leaves in the centre. Break off any flower stems that start to form, but when this happens prepare new seeds and garden beds as the end of the existing plants is nigh.

Silver beet grows happily in most climates all year, though it displays a distinct preference for cool weather as it tends to run to seed in the heat and suffers rust spotting in humid conditions. In ideal conditions silver beet keeps producing new leaves for almost a year and the stem will end up looking like a trunk. It's the ideal cut-and-come-again vegetable.

There is a variety of silver beet known as perpetual spinach that is beautifully leafy and fine-stemmed. It grows very well in a pot as well as in the garden. Don't be deluded by the name 'perpetual', however; it will need replacing in 3-6 months, especially if it's grown in a pot.

Coloured 'rainbow' forms are available with yellow, orange, red and pink stem colours, and ruby chard with red stems alone. They are stunning in the garden and add drama to the dinner plate.

preserving the crop

STORING	Do not wash before storing. Place in a vegetable storage bag in the refrigerator for about 3 days.
FREEZING	Both silver beet and spinach can be blanched and frozen (see Freezing, page 113) for up to 6 months. On thawing you will need to squeeze out all the moisture and they will only be useful in cooked dishes such as pies, soups and casseroles.

spinach

When planting spinach seeds, position them 1cm (½") deep and 15cm (6") apart if planning to harvest leaf by leaf, or 20-30cm (8-12") apart if planning to harvest the whole plant. Closely planted seedlings can be thinned out later. They'll sprout in 2-3 weeks. Mulch well to keep their roots moist and cool and to suppress weeds.

Keep regularly watered and give boosts of liquid fertiliser every month. Both silver beet and spinach also need mulch protection from frosts. You'll be able to pick the outside leaves in about 8 weeks.

Spinach is an easy, cool-season crop, and is happy planted in pots, in clusters or in regimental rows. It grows best during the short days of winter.

Spinach can either be harvested leaf by leaf, or pulled out whole, roots and all. Another method is to cut it off above the soil and the remaining root will obligingly re-shoot to produce a second crop, making it doubly worthwhile.

New Zealand spinach is a wild green that grows naturally along the coast in both Australia and New Zealand. It is also available as seed and will grow anywhere during the warm months, and is most lush when given adequate water. The leaves grow on lanky stems, which are fleshy and mildly flavoured. Harvest a length of stem and strip off the leaves.

for the table

to prepare

• Wash well before using to remove dirt and grit. Wash in a sink of cold water, let the leaves float to the top and then scoop them out. Don't simply let the water drain away as this tends to re-coat the leaves in their grit.

to serve

• Silver beet and spinach can be used interchangeably, but silver beet has a stronger flavour and carries stronger flavours well.

• Mix silver beet, fetta and pine nuts for seasoning a boned leg of lamb.

• The stems of silver beet can be used as a dish on their own. Serve with a strong cheese sauce (with plenty of powdered mustard) and a gratin top.

• Add spinach by the handful to a risotto in the last moments of cooking.

• Combine spinach with ricotta cheese to flavour gnocchi in a rich, cheesy sauce.

• Use both spinach and silver beet leaves to wrap minced chicken and almonds before steaming.

• Deep-fry shredded silver beet and dress with a soy and rice wine dressing with lots of fried garlic, sesame seeds and a tiny sprinkle of sugar.

silver beet

ruby silver beet

rainbow silver beet

spinach

rainbow silver beet with pine nuts, garlic & raisins

1 bunch rainbow silver beet (750g)
2 tablespoons olive oil
1 medium brown onion (150g), chopped finely
2 cloves garlic, crushed
½ cup (85g) raisins
⅓ cup (50g) roasted pine nuts
1 tablespoon lemon juice

1 Separate leaves and stems of silver beet; chop coarsely.

2 Heat half the oil in large pan; cook onion and garlic, stirring, until softened. Add silver beet stems; cook, stirring, until just tender. Add leaves; cook, stirring, until wilted.

3 Remove pan from heat; stir in raisins and half the nuts. Season to taste. Drizzle with lemon juice and remaining oil; sprinkle with remaining nuts.

prep + cook time 20 minutes **serves** 6

spinach soup with fetta

40g butter
1 medium brown onion (150g), chopped coarsely
4 green onions, chopped coarsely
2 cloves garlic, quartered
1 tablespoon coarsely grated lemon rind
1.5kg spinach, trimmed, chopped coarsely
3 large potatoes (900g), chopped coarsely
3 cups (750ml) vegetable stock
5 cups (1.25 litres) water
¾ cup (180ml) pouring cream
150g fetta cheese, crumbled

1 Melt butter in large saucepan; cook both onions and garlic, stirring, until onion softens. Add rind, spinach and potato; cook, stirring, until spinach is just wilted.

2 Stir in stock and the water. Bring to the boil; simmer, covered, about 15 minutes or until the potato softens.

3 Stand 10 minutes then blend or process soup mixture, in batches, until smooth.

4 Return soup with cream to same cleaned pan; stir over heat until hot. Divide soup into serving bowls; top each with cheese.

prep + cook time 40 minutes **serves** 8

citrus fruit

Delightful is the heavy drape of white blooms among lustrous, deep green foliage. During spring, that distinctive citrus perfume pervades the air, and by autumn the branches arch gracefully and bow down laden with fruit. The fruits are filled with juice and bursting with flavour. They are also long lasting, both on the tree and when chilled for storage. When not used for eating fresh or for their juice, the fruits can be used in pickles or chutneys, salted as a condiment or sweetened for marmalades or desserts.

general cultivation

Citrus trees require free-draining soil. Where clay is the base layer or chief component of the soil, the water will drain away too slowly and the roots will rot. To plant a citrus tree in these soils, first apply gypsum to the surface, then follow with a mixture of sand and straw, then raise the soil 30cm (12") with a mixture of rotted manure, sand and compost. Rest this for 2 weeks before planting.

To keep citrus trees in top form, spread a special citrus-blend fertiliser or a combination of pelleted poultry manure and fish-food fertiliser in late winter or early spring and again in late summer. Water in well. The roots lie close to the surface, spreading out to the drip-line of each tree, so avoid disturbing the soil.

Mulch with compost to retain moisture but keep it well clear of the trunk. Apply fertiliser under the drip-line and water in well. Collar rot around the base of the trunk occurs from damp foliage and the build up of too much mulch around the stem. Always keep this area clear and uncongested.

Water regularly for good flower and fruit formation. Don't let roots dry out during long, dry spells. Watering is especially important for trees in pots, and an automatic watering system is very effective.

Most purchased citrus trees are grafted onto hardy, disease-resistant rootstock. Never bury the tree as deep as the graft when planting or adding mulch. Keep a check that new stems don't shoot below the graft as this is the rootstock growing. Vigorous rootstock can rapidly overcome the grafted variety. If growing from seed, make sure to buy 'certified seed' to guarantee the variety you want.

Citrus don't like frosts or exposure to cold gales, and in cold climates they are grown in greenhouses. If grown in pots, they can be moved outdoors in warm weather, but in-ground specimens need wide open greenhouse doorways during the warm weather for air circulation and bees. Protected by a wall or within a courtyard, some citrus varieties cope with light frosts.

Citrus trees, unpruned, assume a neat, compact shape. Lemon trees become open and wide-armed in full sun. Should their spread become too generous, they happily adapt to pruning back into their natural shape.

Hard pruning can be used to re-invigorate an old tree. Cut back to a few short stubs of branches at the main trunk.

Citrus trees can also be pruned as topiary balls at ground level or standardised on self-supporting trunks.

Remember to leave the fruit on the tree until fully ripe and ready to fall as it doesn't ripen after picking.

preserving the crop

STORING	Citrus fruits should be stored in a cool, dry place for up to 3 weeks. Storing in the refrigerator will slightly lengthen their shelf life.
FREEZING	Both the rind and juice freeze well. Remove the rind before freezing and store in plastic containers ready to use. Juice can be frozen in small amounts, such as ice-cube trays, then transferred to freezer bags once frozen (see Freezing, page 113). Freeze juice and rind for up to 6 months. Cumquats and lemons can be frozen whole, packed into rigid freezer containers, for up to 6 months. You will not be able to grate the rind once it has defrosted, but the lemons can still be juiced and the cumquats used as desired. Frozen lemon slices can be added to summer drinks.
PICKLING	All citrus fruits make excellent jams, jellies and marmalades. Pour into hot, sterilised jars and seal while hot (see Bottling, page 114).

oranges

mandarins

cumquat

pests and diseases

Any discolouration or yellowing in the normally glossy evergreen foliage tells you something in the soil is amiss, usually a lack of trace elements. The correct fertiliser regime is called for. The nursery where you bought the plants can diagnose the problem.

Holes eaten into the leaves are a minor problem caused by snails or caterpillars, which can be removed by hand. More disfiguring are leaf miners that make tracks just below the leaf surface and pucker the entire leaf. They can be clipped off or sprayed with white oil mix in late winter and again in summer. Watch for new leaves unfurling and spray immediately.

Aphids will amass on new stems and leaves, and disfigure or kill them. Crush by hand, hose off or spray with an insecticide. A black mould, called sooty mould, can appear on stems and leaves from the honeydew dropped by scale and aphids. Lightly sponge off with warm, soapy water and search for and remove the honeydew producers.

Scales, with their white, pink or brown round waxy coatings or fine desiccated coconut appearance, also mass on the stems of citrus trees. They suck out vital fluids and are very weakening.

Proprietary treatments are available. Alternatively, they can be removed by gently scrubbing with a soft brush.

Fruit fall is another common problem and is usually related to irregular watering. Another reason may be spined citrus bugs, flattened green beetles with horns on either side of their flat heads. They suck from the immature fruits. Treatment is with a proprietary pesticide for crops.

Another visitor is the destructive bronze-orange bug that starts life in winter as a flat, paper-thin beetle. It grows and changes to green then orange. It is easily visible in its final black-bronze stage when it's almost 3cm (1") long, and sucks from the ends of new stems. The stems wilt and the bug squirts a burning liquid with an unpleasant aroma when disturbed. Use a proprietary spray or don rubber gloves and protective glasses and catch them one by one and crush, or dip into a hot water bath to destroy.

in the garden

oranges

Oranges crop for 3-4 months over winter and into spring. Valencia has seeds and a tough skin but is an excellent orange for juice.

Navel oranges are the most popular eating orange with no pips, lots of juice and are easy to peel. They ripen in winter and their bright, vitamin-packed flesh is a real energy booster.

Blood oranges, with their streaky red flesh, are startling when cut, and the bitter 'Seville' orange is excellent for both marmalade and candying.

'Calamondin', a dwarf sweet orange, and 'Chinotto', a bitter one, look good in pots.

lemons

Lemon trees make ideal cook's companions as they are rarely without fruit. During winter the crop is most reliable, ready for marmalades, salting, juicing and freezing. Lemon is the tallest and most rambling member of the citrus troupe but responds happily to pruning and shaping.

'Eureka' is productive all year in mild climates. 'Meyer' is suitable for areas of light frosts and adapts well to pots. 'Lisbon' only crops once a year. A newer cultivar named the lemonade tree has a sweeter, less acidic juice.

limes

yellow grapefruit

ruby grapefruit

limes

Lime trees are more compact than lemons. Most varieties hold some fruit all year, but winter is their peak. They are the most frost-sensitive of all citrus trees. Lime trees require no pruning unless they become misshapen and their pest control regime is the same as for lemons.

mandarins and tangerines

These crop once a year from late autumn to winter. Don't leave the fruit too long before picking as they dry out on the tree. Leave some stem attached if you plan to store them. Easy-to-peel mandarin varieties include 'Imperial' while seedless ones include 'Emperor'. Cross-breeds of mandarin and orange have produced the tangor, while mandarin/grapefruit crosses have produced the tangy tangelo.

grapefruit

That clean, sharp taste is a robust start to the day. Grapefruit appears once a year, in either autumn (wheeny) or winter (marsh seedless). In Britain, 'Golden Special' is prized, and pink and blood grapefruits are becoming a garden must. Grapefruit are prone to fruit-fly attack, so treat as advised (see Pests and Diseases, page 13). Bag the fallen fruit, 'cook' it in the sun, and then dispose of it carefully.

cumquats

These ornamental trees have miniature fruit and leaves. The oval-fruited 'nagami' has fewer seeds and sweet flesh concealed in a thin, bitter skin. 'Marumi' has round fruit and a sharp-flavoured flesh. A variegated form is also available. Cumquats make distinctive marmalade as well as citrus-based liqueurs.

for the table

to prepare

• To remove the rind and pith from thick-rind fruit: top and tail the fruit, then slit the skin from top to bottom. Gently work a spoon under the skin and around the fruit. You will end up with rind ready for making into sweet treats and rind-free fruit ready to cook with or enjoy as they are.

to serve

• There is, of course, their juice to enjoy.

• Serve butter, grated mandarin rind and a little five-spice powder over steamed pak choi.

• Remove the white pith from the rind of your chosen citrus. Make sure the rind is dried thoroughly (see Drying, page 115), then place in jars of caster sugar. Limit yourself to one flavour per jar. After a month the sugar is wonderfully scented with the aroma of the fruit and ready to add to sweet batters.

• Combine avocados, grapefruit segments and butter lettuce; toss with a spicy dressing made with grapefruit juice.

• To add extra zing to casseroles and slow-cooked meats, sprinkle with gremolata (a mixture of garlic, lemon rind and parsley). Excellent with veal, beef or grilled fish.

• Dust plenty of icing sugar onto a cake straight from the oven and squeeze over citrus juice: a good alternative to pouring over a sugar syrup.

• North African recipes often call for preserved lemons. Quarter lemons lengthways and place in sterilised jars (see Bottling, page 114) with salt and sugar; add flavourings such as cinnamon sticks, peppercorns, cumin seeds and bay leaves, and cover the lemons with fresh lemon juice. Keep in the refrigerator for up to 6 months. To use, remove and discard the pulp then rinse the rind. Slice the rind finely and serve over dishes. Note: the juice is not suitable to use as it's too salty.

soba salad with rocket and mandarin

180g soba noodles

2 medium mandarins (400g), segmented, chopped coarsely

2 green onions, sliced thinly

½ cup (80g) roasted pine nuts

40g baby rocket leaves

mandarin vinaigrette

¼ cup (60ml) olive oil

¼ cup (60ml) mandarin juice

1 tablespoon rice wine vinegar

1 Cook noodles in medium pan of boiling water until tender; drain. Rinse under cold water; drain.

2 Meanwhile, make mandarin vinaigrette.

3 Combine noodles and vinaigrette in large bowl with remaining ingredients.

mandarin vinaigrette Combine ingredients in screw-top jar; shake well.

prep + cook time 20 minutes **serves** 6

fennel & ruby red grapefruit salad

2 ruby red grapefruit (700g)

1 medium fennel bulb (300g), trimmed, sliced thinly

2 stalks celery (300g), trimmed, sliced thinly

1 cup loosely packed fresh flat-leaf parsley leaves

¼ cup (25g) roasted walnut halves

white balsamic vinaigrette

¼ cup (60ml) olive oil

1 tablespoon white balsamic vinegar

1 Segment grapefruit over small bowl; reserve 2 tablespoons juice for vinaigrette.

2 Make white balsamic vinaigrette.

3 Combine grapefruit, vinaigrette and remaining ingredients in medium serving bowl.

white balsamic vinaigrette Combine oil, vinegar and reserved juice in screw-top jar; shake well.

prep time 20 minutes **serves** 4

lemon sour cream cake

250g butter, softened

1 tablespoon finely grated lemon rind

2 cups (440g) caster sugar

6 eggs

¾ cup (180g) sour cream

2 cups (300g) plain flour

¼ cup (35g) self-raising flour

½ cup (80g) pine nuts

1 tablespoon demerara sugar

¼ cup (90g) honey, heated

1 Preheat fan oven to 170°C/150°C. Grease deep 23cm-square cake pan; line base and two opposite sides with baking paper, extending paper 5cm over sides.

2 Beat butter, rind and caster sugar in bowl with electric mixer until light and fluffy. Add eggs, one at a time, beating until combined (mixture may separate at this stage, but will come together later). Stir in sour cream and sifted flours, in two batches. Spread mixture into pan; bake 15 minutes.

3 Combine nuts and demerara sugar in small bowl.

4 Remove cake from oven; sprinkle evenly with nut mixture, press gently into cake. Bake a further 45 minutes. Stand cake in pan 5 minutes before turning, top-side up, onto wire rack. Drizzle hot cake evenly with hot honey; cool before serving.

prep + cook time 1 hour 15 minutes (+ cooling)
serves 16

ever-lasting orange slices

These orange slices can be used in trifles, cake fillings, as cheesecake toppings or even squeezed into split croissants for a special breakfast. They will keep in the refrigerator for up to 6 months.

12 medium oranges (2kg)

10 cups (2.5 litres) water

8 cups (1.75kg) caster sugar

¾ cup (180ml) orange-flavoured liqueur

1 Bring very large pan of salted water to the boil; add whole oranges. Return to the boil; drain, rinse under cold water. Repeat twice more. Cut oranges into 5-7mm (¼") thick slices, remove seeds.

2 Combine the water and sugar in same pan. Stir over heat until sugar is dissolved; do not boil. Add orange slices; simmer about 2 hours or until orange slices are soft and very shiny. Stir in liqueur. Gently spoon slices into hot sterilised jars; seal while hot.

prep + cook time 3 hours

note If you have a lot of syrup left over, you can bottle some separately to spoon over cakes or flavour creams.

winter herbs

The perennial herbs available in the winter enjoy an uncanny sympathy with the foods we crave when the nights turn cold and dark: roasts, soups and all those dishes that require long, slow cooking, drawing out the flavours and filling the house with rich scents and fireside warmth. Summer seems a long way off, and winter herbs capture that absent sunshine.

in the garden

bay leaves

Bay is one of the few tree herbs. And what a tree. It's not choosy about soils or climate and it can reach 11m (35') and spread almost as wide. A bay tree is more suited to a large garden or park rather than a herb patch, but it adapts to topiary shaping and is often standardised as feature points in the centre or corners of a formal garden. Bay also grows well in a pot, and can be espaliered as a hedge, fence or border.

The leathery evergreen leaves are used to flavour casseroles, milk sauces, marinades and stocks. Dry and store in an airtight container. The leaves can be used fresh, but some people insist the flavour is stronger when dried.

Watch for brown scale on the leaves because en masse they can weaken a small tree. Lightly scrub them off with soapy water or use a proprietary spray.

thyme

This low-growing herb is excellent in the garden as a edging, in clumps among rocks or in pots. It needs full sun and gritty, free-draining soil to thrive. It will rot in damp, shady sites. It grows to about 30cm (12") but it usually masses on itself and leans over and sets roots. Cut it back when it becomes too unmanageable and use the new rooted plants as replacements every couple of years.

There are many leaf forms and varieties which are used fresh and dried. Lemon thyme goes particularly well with veal and mushrooms. Its scent is due to the high level of citral found in its leaves, an oil also found in lemon, orange, verbena and lemon grass. The citrus scent is enhanced by crushing the leaves in your hands before using the herb.

Add thyme at the beginning of cooking so the flavours meld. Pull off the small leaves if you don't want to serve them with their stringy stems.

marjoram

Marjoram is a relative of oregano (their flavours also are similar). It grows lower at about 30cm (12") and its spread is more of a mound. Marjoram will sulk and disappear in shady spots and needs protection from cold winter winds. It is well suited to life in a pot. Prune back hard at the end of summer and collect the trimmings to dry.

Marjoram is most often teamed with other herbs and very rarely used by itself in recipes. It goes well with tomato-based dishes, and the dried stems burned on the barbecue adds a nice tang to the food. It has small, soft grey-green leaves with a slightly earthy, distinctive flavour, which is sweeter and milder than oregano. Oregano, while known as wild marjoram, has larger, thicker stems and darker leaves that have a more pungent, peppery flavour.

Marjoram, along with bay leaves, thyme and parsley, are the traditional herbs of a bouquet garni, often added to slow-cooked soups and casseroles.

preserving the crop

STORING	Store fresh herbs in damp paper towel in vegetable storage bags in the refrigerator for up to 3 days.
FREEZING	Bay leaves, thyme, marjoram and sage all freeze well. Freeze in small containers for up to 6 months (see Freezing, page 113). They don't need to be chopped before freezing; freeze in a covered tray with their stems intact. Frozen, the leaves are easily removed to use.
DRYING	All the winter herbs can be dried and stored in airtight containers for several months (see Drying, page 115). Hang bunches decoratively around the kitchen.

sage

There are handsome purple-flushed and yellow-variegated sages available as well as the usual grey. Sage grows about 30cm (12") high, doesn't grow in acidic soil and will collapse with too much rain. Add grit to the soil if you've had failures before, and confinement to a well-drained pot will reduce 'wet feet' syndrome. Watch for caterpillars as they'll strip the leaves in no time.

Its deep blue salvia flowers appear in summer, but for profuse leaves, snip off the stems as the flowers form.

The flavour of sage is strong, fresh or dried, so use sparingly. The intense flavour suits strongly-flavoured, rich, fatty meat dishes such as pork and duck. It is the herb of choice in many stuffings including the traditional sage and onion stuffing often found in Christmas turkeys.

for the table

to serve

• Cook crumbed lamb cutlets in butter and oil; remove from the pan and add lemon juice, thyme and more butter. Serve the butter sauce over the lamb.

• Squeeze lemon juice and sprinkle chopped fresh marjoram over potatoes before roasting. The smell and flavour are both delicious.

• Place a sage leaf and a piece of mozzarella in the centre of a pork schnitzel; fold into parcels, secure with string then dust in flour and cook in butter and olive oil until golden and cooked through. Remove the string before serving.

classic herb blends These include *bouquet garni* and *herbes de Provence*, and are used to flavour stocks, soups, sauces, stews and casseroles. They are tied together in a small bundle using unwaxed kitchen string, or placed in a small muslin (cheesecloth) bag, which is removed before serving.

A bouquet garni usually consists of 2-3 springs of parsley, 1 sprig thyme, 1-2 bay leaves; other herbs may then be added according to local region. For additional flavour, try adding sage, rosemary, lemon peel and whole black peppercorns.

Herbes de Provence includes thyme, marjoram and bay leaves, as well as rosemary, fennel, mint oregano and tarragon. This blend can be used with either fresh or dried herbs, and orange zest and lavender are sometimes included. The dry blend is good mixed with olive oil to coat meat, chicken or fish; the fresh blend is used in soups, stews and tossed over vegetables before roasting.

for the pantry

• Bay leaves are said to ward off weevils so scatter through your pantry. Even if this doesn't work, the leaves will add a wonderful scent to the shelves.

bay leaves

thyme

marjoram

sage

braised pork with fresh sage

90g butter

1.5kg rack of pork (6 cutlets), rind removed

2 medium carrots (240g), sliced thickly

6 baby onions (150g), peeled

4 cloves garlic, peeled

2 bay leaves

6 sprigs fresh thyme

1⅓ cups (330ml) white wine

⅓ cup (80ml) white wine, extra

⅓ cup (80ml) chicken stock

1 tablespoon sage leaves

1 Preheat fan oven to 180°C/160°C.

2 Melt butter in large, flameproof dish in stove top; cook pork until browned, remove from dish.

3 Add carrots, onions, garlic, bay leaves and thyme to dish. Stir over heat 5 minutes or until beginning to brown. Return pork to dish with wine. Transfer to oven; cook about 1¼ hours or until cooked as desired. Remove pork; cover keep warm.

4 Strain cooking liquid into small saucepan; discard vegetables. Add extra wine and stock to pan; bring to the boil. Reduce heat; simmer 5 minutes. Stir in sage. Serve pork with sage sauce, and roasted baby new potatoes and baby truss tomatoes, if you like.

prep + cook time 1 hour 45 minutes **serves** 6

note Ask your butcher to remove the rind and tie the pork well. Roast the salted rind on a rack in a hot oven until crisp. Serve with the pork.

roasted thyme potatoes with spicy sauce

500g baby new potatoes, halved

2 tablespoons olive oil

1 tablespoon finely chopped fresh thyme

spicy sauce

1 tablespoon olive oil

1 small brown onion (80g), chopped finely

2 cloves garlic, sliced thinly

1 fresh small red Thai chilli, chopped finely

410g can crushed tomatoes

2 teaspoons caster sugar

1 Preheat fan oven to 220°C/200°C.

2 Combine potatoes, oil and thyme in large baking dish; roast about 30 minutes or until potato is tender.

3 Meanwhile, make spicy sauce.

4 Serve spicy sauce with hot roasted potatoes.

spicy **sauce** Heat oil in medium pan; cook onion, garlic and chilli, stirring occasionally, until onion is soft. Add undrained tomatoes and sugar; bring to the boil. Simmer, uncovered, stirring occasionally, about 10 minutes or until sauce thickens.

prep + cook time 45 minutes **serves** 8

preserving your crop

One danger of successful gardening is sheer over-abundance. What do you do with kilos of courgettes? Mint gone mad? Too many beans? One of the delights of too-successful gardening is preserving the crop, giving away what you don't need, storing for winter, making gifts, and enjoying last year's raspberries, plums and tomatoes as this year's jams, marmalades and preserves. Here we provide general guidelines on simple home-preservation techniques. Always choose the best, the ripest and the least blemished of your fruit and vegetables – so don't leave preserving until the end of the season or you'll miss the best of your crop.

freezing

Containers must be airtight. Shallow dishes allow food to freeze and thaw more quickly. Containers must be microwave-safe if you plan to microwave from the freezer. Always allow cooked food to cool completely before freezing. Food expands as it freezes so allow 2-5cm (1-2") extra space in containers.

Use labels to record the contents, freezing date and quantity, and use a waterproof pen.

Ice-cube trays are the perfect-sized containers for freezing small quantities of chopped herbs, chopped chillies and grated ginger. Each compartment holds about 1 tablespoon. Some herbs may need a little water to cling together. Once frozen, transfer the cubes to a container or bag. Each time you need the flavouring, add a cube.

Sprigs of herbs can be crumbled while still frozen. Basil, oregano, mint and coriander freeze well. Once frozen, herbs are only useful in cooked dishes or salad dressings, not as salad ingredients.

To blanch vegetables before freezing, drop them into a large pan of boiling water and allow the water to return to the boil. Drain immediately and plunge into a large bowl (or sink) of iced water until cold. Drain well before packing into freezer containers. If blanching large quantities, check the temperature of the iced water as it does warm up. Add more iced water, if necessary.

Frozen stone fruit, apples, pears, plums and oranges make quick desserts. Poach in a light sugar syrup with spices and freeze in rigid containers to keep their shape. To serve, thaw and spoon over ice-cream or freshly baked plain cakes.

bottling

Old-fashioned bottling requires a bottling kit, a set of instructions and years of experience. Some practitioners have turned bottling into an art (visit any country show), but the technique is complex and not for the beginner or those rushed for time. If you want to try bottling, seek the help of a friend or relative with experience in this method of preservation.

Making preserves (jam, pickles, chutneys, relishes) is a much simpler alternative to bottling. The added sugar and vinegar act as preservation agents, lessening the need for precise temperatures and heating times. Follow our instructions for sterilising and sealing bottles and preserving will be easy.

Successful preservation requires still-warm, sterilised bottles, warm preserves and rapid sealing.

You'll need plenty of glass jars or bottles. They must have no chips or cracks and be thoroughly scrubbed clean. Choose bottles with airtight, coated metal lids. Uncoated lids will corrode. Snap-on and screw-top plastic lids do not seal tightly enough.

sterilising jars

Remember, the lids also need to be sterilised along with the bottles.

There are three main methods of home sterilisation. Once sterilised, remove each jar carefully and turn upside-down onto a clean tea towel on a wooden board. Turn upright only when ready to use.

By far, the easiest method is to put the jars and lids in the dishwasher on the hottest rinse cycle available. Don't use detergent.

The second method is boiling. Lay the jars and lids in a large pan, cover completely with cold water and bring gradually to the boil; boil for 20 minutes.

The last method is in the oven. Place the jars and lids, upright, but not touching, on a clean wooden board. Place the board in a cold oven and turn the oven temperature to very low (120°C/150°F) for 30 minutes.

sealing jars

Sealing the jars is as important as sterilising them. Once you've filled the jars, seal them immediately. The sooner the jars are sealed, the less likely their contents will spoil.

Paper, cellophane and foil are not suitable sealants. Cellophane and paper are not airtight and foil

corrodes with any acids in the preserves. Brown paper can be used as an extra sealant. When you have placed the lids on the jars, cut out a large circle of brown paper, coat with glue and place over the lids and wrap down the sides of the jar to form a tight seal.

If you don't have enough lids, use paraffin wax. It is available from larger supermarkets and chemists and creates an excellent seal. Melt the wax over very low heat. Pour a thin layer over the preserves and allow to set. Next, pour over another layer of wax, this time including a piece of string to help you pull out the wax to open. Don't overheat the wax or it will shrink when it sets and not form a complete seal.

labelling jars

Don't kid yourself you'll remember that the apple and date chutney has the green lid and the tomato cumin relish is in the tall thin bottle. Label with contents and preserving date.

Store preserves in a cool, dark place and leave for a week or so before opening. All preserves taste better when left to rest. In hot, humid climates, the best place to store them is the refrigerator. Once opened, all preserves must be stored, covered, in the refrigerator.

drying

sun-drying

Tomatoes, apples, pears, apricots, peaches and chillies are all good to dry. You need 4-5 days of constant sun with little or no humidity. (Beware: in humid conditions a mould develops very quickly.) Don't be disappointed if the fruit changes colour as it dries; its taste is not affected. Commercially dried fruits have ascorbic acid and sulphur added to retain their colour. It's not necessary to peel fruit before drying, but as drying can make the skin leathery (apples and apricots in particular), you may wish to peel some fruits.

You will need wooden or non-corrosive racks with rungs close enough together to stop the food falling through (as it shrinks greatly), but not too close to disrupt the airflow.

Thicker fruits, such as apples and pears, need to be sliced; most other fruits just need halving. Place the fruit, cut-side up, on the racks, place the racks over a tray and cover with fine wire mesh (not touching the fruit). Clean fly-screens are ideal. Position in the hottest, sunniest place you can find.

It's a good idea to bring the trays inside or into an airy shed at night so they're not disturbed by animals, and so dew won't rehydrate the fruit and make it go mouldy.

The fruit is dry when no moisture oozes when it is cut. Store fruit in airtight containers in a cool place for 6 months. Of course, label as you go.

air-drying

Fresh herbs and chillies can be air-dried. Hang bunches in an airy place or on racks covered with absorbent paper, away from direct sunlight to retain as much flavour as possible.

microwave-drying

You can dry herbs in a microwave oven, if you like, between several sheets of absorbent paper on HIGH (100%) for about 1 minute. If not dry, repeat, checking every 30 seconds (sometimes the paper will need to be changed). Label and store in airtight containers.

oven-drying

All fruits that can be sun-dried can also be oven-dried – especially tomatoes. Prepare the fruit on racks as for sun-drying (without the fly-screen).

A good drying oven temperature is about 50°C (120°F). Tomatoes need a higher temperature to dry out their extra juice. Don't hurry the process or you will spoil the fruit. You may need more than a day, so place as much fruit in the oven as you can. You can dry different fruits together. Once the fruit is dried, let it cool before storing in airtight containers.

Herbs dry very well in the oven and take little space and time (about 20 minutes), so are ideal to do in batches along with other fruit. That excess of chillies can be oven-dried as well.

glossary

BICARBONATE OF SODA also known as baking or carb soda.

BREADCRUMBS

packaged fine-textured, crunchy, purchased white breadcrumbs.

stale one- or two-day-old bread made into crumbs by blending or processing.

BUTTER use salted or unsalted butter; 125g equals one stick (4 ounces).

CHEESE

cream commonly known as Philly or Philadelphia, a soft cows'-milk cheese.

fetta a crumbly goat- or sheep-milk cheese with a sharp salty taste.

goat's made from goat's milk; has an earthy, strong taste. Available in soft and firm textures, in various shapes and sizes; may be rolled in ash or herbs.

mascarpone fresh, unripened, smooth, triple cream cheese with a rich, sweet, slightly acidic, taste.

Parmesan also known as parmigiana; a hard, grainy cows'-milk cheese.

CREAM we used fresh cream, also known as pouring cream.

sour a cultured soured cream.

FLOUR

plain an all-purpose flour made from wheat. **Wholemeal plain flour** is also known as all-purpose wholewheat flour; it has no baking powder added. Flour is milled from the whole wheat grain (bran, germ and endosperm).

self-raising plain flour sifted with baking powder (the ratio being 1 cup flour to 2 teaspoons baking powder).

FRENCH-STYLE CRÊPES pre-cooked, thin, French style crêpes; suitable for both sweet or savoury dishes. Available in the freezer section of most supermarkets.

GARAM MASALA a blend of spices including cardamom, cinnamon, cloves, coriander, fennel and cumin. Black pepper and chilli add extra heat.

MAPLE SYRUP, PURE thin syrup distilled from the sap of the maple tree. Maple-flavoured syrup or pancake syrup is not an adequate substitute.

MINCE also known as ground meat.

MIRIN a Japanese cooking wine; made of glutinous rice and alcohol and used expressly for cooking. Should not be confused with sake.

PAPRIKA a ground dried sweet red pepper (capsicum); there are many types available, including sweet, hot, mild and smoked.

PINE NUTS also known as pignoli; not in fact a nut, but a small, cream-coloured kernel from pine cones.

PITTA BREAD flat, unleavened bread of Mediterranean origin.

PROSCIUTTO cured, air-dried, pressed ham; usually sold thinly sliced.

RAISINS dried sweet grapes.

RICE, JASMINE fragrant long-grained rice; white rice can be substituted, but will not taste the same.

SALT, SEA SALT FLAKES unrefined salt available in both fine and coarse grains from most supermarkets. Made from evaporated sea water.

SAUCES

chilli, hot we use a hot Chinese variety made from red Thai chillies, salt and vinegar. Use sparingly, increasing the quantity to suit your taste.

fish (nam pla or nuoc nam); made from pulverised salted fermented fish, most often anchovies. Has a pungent smell and strong taste; so use sparingly.

oyster a rich, brown sauce made from oysters and their brine, cooked with salt and soy sauce, and thickened with starches.

soy also known as sieu, is made from fermented soya beans.

Japanese an all-purpose low-sodium soy sauce made with more wheat content than its Chinese counterparts. Possibly the best table soy and the one to choose if you only want one variety.

light a fairly thin, pale but salty tasting soy sauce; used in dishes in which the natural colour of the ingredients is to be maintained. Not to be confused with salt-reduced or low-sodium soy sauces.

SESAME SEEDS available in both black and white; white seeds have a nutty flavour, while the black seeds taste more bitter. Store in the fridge, as they can go rancid in hot weather.

SUGAR

brown soft, finely granulated sugar retaining molasses for its colour and flavour. Available as both light and dark.

caster also known as superfine or finely granulated table sugar.

icing sugar also known as powered sugar or confectioners' sugar; granulated sugar crushed together with a small amount of cornflour.

white a coarsely granulated table sugar, also known as crystal sugar.

TOFU, FIRM made by compressing bean curd to remove most of the water. Good used in stir-fries because it can be tossed without falling apart.

TURMERIC, GROUND also known as kamin; a member of the ginger family, its root is dried and ground, resulting in the rich yellow powder used to give dishes their characteristic colour. It is intensely pungent in taste but not hot.

VINEGAR

balsamic made from Trebbiano grape juice; it is a deep, rich brown colour with a sweet and sour flavour.

balsamic white vinegar (condiment) a clear, lighter version of balsamic vinegar; has a fresh, sweet clean taste.

raspberry made from fresh raspberries steeped in a white wine vinegar.

red wine based on fermented red wine.

rice wine made from rice wine lees (the sediment left after fermentation), salt and alcohol.

white made from spirit of cane sugar.

white wine made from a blend of white wines.

index

If you like this cool book, you'll love these...

These are just a small selection of titles available. The Australian Women's Weekly range is on sale at selected newsagents and supermarkets or online at **www.australian-womens-weekley.com**

This book is published in 2011 by Octopus Publishing Group Limited

based on materials licensed to it by ACP Magazines Ltd, a division of PBL Media Pty Limited

acp
books

54 Park St, Sydney

GPO Box 4088, Sydney, NSW 2001
phone (02) 9282 8618;

fax (02) 9267 9438

acpbooks@acpmagazines.com.au;
www.acpbooks.com.au

International foreign language rights, Brian Cearnes, ACP Books bcearnes@ acpmagazines.com.au

OCTOPUS BOOKS

UK Editor – Helen Griffin

Published and Distributed in the United Kingdom by Octopus Publishing Group Limited

Endeavour House

189 Shaftesbury Avenue
London WC2H 8JY
United Kingdom
phone + 44 (0) 207 632 5400;
fax + 44 (0) 207 632 5405

aww@octopusbooks.co.uk;
www.octopusbooks.co.uk

www.australian-womens-weekly.com

Printed and bound in China.

A catalogue record for this book is available from the British Library.
ISBN **978-1-90742-829-6**
© ACP Magazines Ltd 2010

ABN 18 053 273 546

To order Australian Women's Weekly books:
telephone LBS on 01903 828 503
or order online at
www.australian-womens-weekly.com
or www.octopusbooks.co.uk